YOU BRANDING

REINVENTING YOUR PERSONAL IDENTITY
AS A SUCCESSFUL BRAND

MARK CIJO
FOREWORD BY MIKE ATACK

Printed by CreateSpace

An Amazon.com Company

Every other book you read till this date might be dedicated to someone else - The author's dad, wife, ex , colleague, son or what ever. This book is dedicated to you.

Even though you don't know me, we haven't met or facebooked, I trust you are a possibility thinker and want to succeed in life. That's why you are here.

This one is for you!

CONTENTS

Define Your Values
Ask for Help
What Do You Enjoy? What are Your Strengths?
How Are You Unique?
Examine the External and the Internal
Do the SWOT Test
Dealing with Your Weaknesses
Make the Changes and Build Your Brand the Right Way

Whom Do You Want to Reach?
Looking for Prospective Employers
Targeting Customers and Clients
Easy Ways to Research All Your Targets
Using the Web and Offline Methods for Research
Something to Keep in Mind
What Makes Your Target Come to You?
Developing Your Message
Focus on Your Benefits as a Brand
Embrace Social Media Fully
Know Your Message Goals
Some Parting Tips to Help Your Aim

How Do You Define Your Specialty or Niche?

Being Too Pushy
Not Being Social
Incomplete Profiles
Not Linking
Lack of Focus in Your Messages
Lack of Humility

Keep Up with the Times and Tech
Keep Looking at the Competition
Take on the Best Projects
Create New Goals
Nurture Your Audience

Back to Google
Real Change and a Powerful Brand

ACKNOWLEDGEMENT

Thanks to…

God Almighty.

My lovely wife Sinu Philipose, who supported me during the writing and research of this book.

My parents, friends and colleagues who extended their sincere support during the course of writing.

My first kid "brawnycode", Co-Founder and my best friend Arun Joseph.

Aravind Ramesh for his help in proofreading the book.

My designer Zizi Iryaspraha S for all his hard work in the Design and Layout of this book.

John Harapkov, Mark Michuda, Randy Lesciralli & Erdal Gull, you guys know how much your support and friendship meant to me.

All my clients and mentors.

FOREWORD

It is a pleasure to be asked to introduce this book to you. I have been a leadership coach for over 18 years, have delivered over 175 talking presentations and have had personally coached with over 1,2500 individuals, among them CEOs, MDs and Directors. As such, I appreciate the importance of Personal Branding.

Your personal brand can be your greatest asset. With the help of this book, you will learn to understand the intricacies of personal branding as it takes you step by step through the process of transforming your identity into a successful personal brand.

I have known Mark for a couple of years and have been able to witness how he has applied personal branding in his own career. There have been moments when I see traits of my personality reflected in Mark; from his insights into how to achieve success, to his ability to build for himself a strong brand. I have had the pleasure to work with him and admire him fo writing a book such as this. Mark is well equipped to walk you through the process of transforming your identity into a strong personal brand.

Not only does this book aim to teach you, it also seeks to inspire. By using the examples of highly successful companies and incorporating the stories behind world famous personal brands, this book will help you learn the ins and outs of personal branding.

This book may well prove to be one of the most important tools you could have on your journey to creating a successful personal brand. It will not only help you identify your strengths, but also your Unique Selling Points and your target. It will help you discover and create ways to continue building and focusing on your skills. This book contains a multitude of techniques and tools to help you create your brand and promote it.

This book will prove to be a great read for you and I have every confidence that it will assist you in reinventing yourself as a successful personal brand.

I wish you luck on your journey with Mark. Happy reading.

Mike Atack

Founder and Managing Director of 8ack International

Introduction to Personal Branding

> **❝***Personal branding is about managing your name — even if you don't own a business — in a world of misinformation, disinformation, and semi-permanent Google records. Going on a date? Chances are that your "blind" date has Googled your name. Going to a job interview? Ditto.* **❞**
>
> - Tim Ferriss
> Author of The
> 4-Hour Work
> Week

Personal branding is nothing new, but more and more people today are starting to see the benefits it can confer. Whether you are trying to get a better job in your current company, or you are looking to find a job with a new employer, or you are trying to boost the level of recognition you have from your audience, personal branding is the way to do it.

In this book, I will cover all of the different aspects of building your own brand. I will do my best to demystify the path to creating a great personal brand that can really make a difference in your life.

To Those Who Bought This Book

I'd like to take a moment to personally thank you for buying this book. It's my sincere desire to make sure you have the knowledge and the tools to get ahead in today's world, and to make sure you are always putting your best foot forward – even when you let the digital world do most of the talking for you.

I want to mentor you through creating your own powerful personal brand. Even if you don't know anything about branding right now, by the time you finish with this book, you will have the expertise to handle your branding and to get your message out into the world.

Take a Moment to Google Your Name

Have you ever used Google to look yourself up? If you are like most people, then you can't help but be curious about what the great and powerful Google has to say about you. Whether you've used the search engine to look yourself up before or not, it's time that you do that now for the purposes of this book.

Go ahead and take a moment to enter your name into the search engine. I'll wait.

Are you back? Great!

What pops up first? Do you even show up at all? What does the world have to say about you? What do your social networks have to say to anyone else who might Google you?

Just as Tim Ferriss's quote says, *everyone* is going to Google your name – first dates, friends, potential employers, and more. You had better hope they find some good stuff on there!

By the time you finish with this book and start to apply all of the tools and the steps you find, you will have much better control of your branding. You will control how the world sees you and what it sees when they look you up in the search engines.

As you will see, branding can play a huge role in your life and the successes you achieve. Without proper branding, you will not be able to realize your full potential. I'll make sure you know what you are doing.

In the End

At the end of the book, once you've incorporated all of these things into your branding efforts, I'll have you run another Google search. If you've done everything in the book and you were diligent about it, you should start to see the big difference. The results that pop up will be the ones *you* always wanted. They are the ones that can show you in your best light.

You Can Do This!

What are you waiting for? Get started carving your brand today, so you can reach the level of personal and professional success you deserve! It's not hard to do, and this book provides you with the tools you need to manage your brand identity.

4

> **❝** *Life isn't about finding your-self. Life is about creating your-self* **❞**
> George Bernhard Shaw,
> Author

CHAPTER
1

Why is Personal Branding Important?

Most people today, whether they are in business or not, know what a brand is. The term is more than merely a buzzword, and more than just businesses are able to see the benefits proper branding can provide.

Of course, you may be wondering if it really matters that you develop or even care about your own personal brand. The truth is, in the ultra-connected and always-online world of today, nurturing and growing your brand is actually very important.

We All Know Brands

Even if you aren't up to date on all of the latest trends in business and in modern life, you still know brands and the concept of branding, thanks to all of the large companies and corporations that employ branding strategies. Consider some of the most powerful brands in the market today:

- ✅ Apple
- ✅ Coca-Cola,
- ✅ McDonald's
- ✅ Google
- ✅ IBM
- ✅ Microsoft

Chances are good you know these companies and their logos, as well as what the businesses do and offer. This is no accident, nor is it good luck on the company's part! These businesses have been perfecting their branding and marketing skills for a number of years. They change and tweak their marketing and branding to find out what works and discard what doesn't.

While branding a company is different from branding an individual, you will find there are actually quite a few similarities. Knowing some of the things that can work well for business branding really can help you with your personal branding too.

The History of Personal Branding

As I mentioned earlier, personal branding is not new at all. While there are actually quite a few new tools in use today, such as social media and other applications, branding has been around for ages. In fact, you can trace personal branding back more than seventy years.

Napoleon Hill

It was in 1937 that one of the seminal works of personal and professional enrichment came into the world. Think and Grow Rich by Napoleon Hill was the first work to include personal branding for financial gain. The book, which has sold more than twenty million copies since publication, goes into personal branding and positioning, as well as how those things can help a person to achieve more success and ultimately more wealth.

You have probably heard of the following statement:

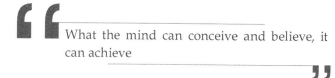

> What the mind can conceive and believe, it can achieve

This comes from Hill's book, and it has a much deeper truth to it than any new age self-help book or guru might be able to offer. It simply means that having clear and firm beliefs, and taking the right steps to achieve those beliefs and desires, make achieving that success far more likely.

He believed that those who did not have a clear plan and who did not have clear beliefs were not going to find the same success – at least not without a lot of luck. That certainly holds true today, and part of the plan of success is personal branding.

Jack Trout and Al Reis

While Hill's book sold well, there wasn't really another large push to expound on personal branding until the early 1980s. Their book, Positioning, the Battle for Your Mind, delved deeper into self-positioning as well as just how important it was. They felt that it was important to find a position or paradigm to latch onto and to make your own, and that's very similar to what you will find with today's version of personal branding on the web.

Networking Then and Now

Networking was just as important back then as it is now. The biggest difference is that most of the networking back then happened over lunches, at office parties, at conventions, and over drinks. While that is still true today to some extent, the majority of networking today is possible to accomplish online.

In addition to the changes in the way you can position yourself today, there also seems to be a change in the dynamic between employer and employee. The two are generally far closer today than they once were, at least in terms of their knowledge of one another. A huge part of that reason is the wealth of information that's out there and online about everyone.

Times Change

Times changed, and the traditional idea of work and employment changed. Years ago, it was possible to work for one company your entire life and you could be relatively sure of your job security. By positioning your personal brand well within that company, and branding within that setting, it was possible to rise through the ranks.

Economic security was no sure thing though. Changes in the times meant that the traditional concept of work has to change as well. People started to want more from their jobs than just money. They also wanted to be happy with the work they were doing.

This meant they needed to start looking for jobs that suited them better, and they needed to have something that made them special and unique so they could stand out from the crowd. Personal branding was the answer to that.

The tools available today will make your branding efforts much easier than they were for people in the past, and that's some great news! It allows you to put your own destiny in your hands, and that's exactly where it should be.

More than Jobs and Corporate Culture

One of the myths of personal branding is that it only applies to corporations and other types of employment settings. Even though that might be what most people think when they imagine branding, it goes well beyond that.

In this book, I will reflect on that by covering different uses and reasons to perfect your personal branding.

The more you look into personal branding, the easier it is to see just how influential it is in so many different areas of your life. Creating a good and likeable image is important for every facet of your life – not just your job, and that's just what Tim Ferriss says in the opening quote to this book.

Personal Branding is Important for Everyone

Regardless of your field, regardless of your position, and regardless of where you want to take your life, proper personal branding is a way to help ensure your success. Whether you are a student fresh out of school and looking for your big break, or you have been in the workforce for a number of years and you are on the job hunt for something new and exciting, personal branding can work for you.

Traditional Career Paradigm – A New Reality

Authors, actors, real estate pros, graphic designers, investment professionals and everyone in between can benefit from building their own brand and managing their reputation online and offline.

Fortunately, the technology of today makes it far easier to control one's personal brand than it was in the past.

Traditionally, when you would try to find work, you would submit a resume and go in for an interview. You could excel at the interview, and if you had the right experience, you had a good chance of landing in the job.

Today, things are quite a bit different. Thanks to the same types of technology thatyou use to browse the web and to keep up with your friends on social media sites, your employers and those you hope to hire you can find out quite a bit about you.

Employers and prospective employers today will use Google and social media when they are calling you in for an interview to learn as much as they can about you and what you can offer their company. They want to see what types of information might be out there about you.

If there are any red flags or some information that might paint you in an unflattering light, you need to get a handle on it. You have to know what types of materials are out there, and you need to know how you can put your best foot forward to improve your chances.

People and employers will look at the personal brand you've already built up, even if you did not know you were building a brand at the time.

The things you do and say online can follow you around and haunt you. If you have a lot of negative information on the web, chances are you will not get the job you want. You have to learn to control this info and determine what the potential employer sees.

Alternatively, the results in the search engine can actually help you when you brand right. When you take full control and responsibility of your personal brand, you can have more control over how people view you. This gives you a huge advantage.

How Does the Paradigm Shift?

As we've mentioned, the world today is far different from what it once was for the employed person, or anyone for that matter.

Let's take a much closer look at how these changes are affecting the workforce of today.

Number One: The Old School Traditional Career

Instead of having just a single job from the time you first start your career to the time you retire things today are vastly different. It used to be that you could find one company and stay with it until retirement.

Those companies appreciated the loyalty and the dedication of the employees, and they rewarded those employees with good benefits, a pension, and a steady job. Companies back then had more stability than the companies today have. This security, along with the benefits, was able to keep most of the employees satisfied.

Today, thanks to uncertainty in the economy, along with a greater desire of employees to find jobs they actually like, employees want more. They want to advance in their careers, and if they can't do that in their current company, they will look for new employment. In fact, many employees will change their employer after two or three years.

Number Two: Fulltime and Permanent

The world is quickly becoming a freelance-centric place. It is more difficult to find those dream jobs that will be steady for twenty or thirty years. Companies today are too unstable, thanks to economic changes, changes in technology, and buyouts from larger companies and conglomerates.

Employees are in a near constant state of unease because they never know when the next layoff might be creeping up on them. They never know when the company might have to downsize.

This has helped to change the way employees think about their jobs. It doesn't mean that you aren't loyal to your company while you are there. It simply means that you need to be thinking about tomorrow and the next day rather than only what is happening right now. You have to look out for yourself.

Positioning your personal brand and keeping watch on other opportunities out there that might make excellent potential employers is the name of the game today. Think about your career as though you are a free agent. It is always in your best interest to look for new and better opportunities.

Those who have the ability to work in a freelance capacity may wish to use their personal branding position to assist them with their freelancing career. Having a backup plan is always smart, and the ability to freelance can help you get by even if your company does have a layoff.

Number Three: New Ways to Find Work

In the past, it was difficult to know exactly where all of those potential jobs were. Most of the time, those who were looking for a new job had to look on job boards and in classified ads. They would have been able to find some leads through friends who were in similar careers.

You would send out your resume and hope that the people who received it would realize what an asset you could be. However, even the best resume writers can't compete with the tools and tech of today.

You have many new ways to find work today, including the web. The web is home to a host of ways to look for work, including job boards and classifieds. However, that's just the start. You can do more than simply seek out jobs on the web though.

You can position yourself on the web to get the type of career you want to have. By blogging and becoming involved with social networking, you can put out much more about you than you could ever get across in a simple CV.

By building your online presence, you can brand yourself as exactly the type of person any company would want to hire and bring onboard. The employers might actually start coming to you!

Number Four: Learning New Skills

In the past, you might have been able to get by with a small but valuable skill set. While it is still good to have a strong skill set, you can bet that everyone else in your particular career has that same skill set. In fact, you might find you are competing against hundreds of other people who will have the exact set of skills.

In the past, this was the norm. Today, you need to offer much more if you want to have a chance at getting the job you really want to have.

What is it that makes you different? What other skills do you bring to the table? These things will definitely help you in your career search. By ensuring that you are keeping up with the latest changes in your field, and adding other skills to your repertoire, you can show employers you have more to offer. Always be as close to the cutting-edge in your field as possible.

By tailoring your personal branding to reflect your skills, as well as all of the things that make you unique and better than the competition, you can start to stand out from the crowd.

Number Five: You are in Charge

Another one of the big changes in the traditional career paradigm is how your career affects your future. In the past, you would generally stay at a single company, and there was usually just a single path to the top.

Now, you are in charge of your own career, and that means you have more choices. You are the one who gets to determine what you want to do next and where you want to go.

Of course, you do need to be aware of just how the choices you are making will affect your overall career path, and you need to make sure your brand reflects who you are and what you want to become.

Overall, the days of being a faceless drone in the crowd are over. The web and social networking help to make it possible for each person to become an individual and to use that individuality to reach new heights in your career. I'll show you methods you can use to harness the power of the web to your advantage.

Why is Job Satisfaction Important?

I've touched briefly on job satisfaction thus far, but it's time I layout why it is so important. The satisfaction you feel from your job – or the dissatisfaction as the case may be – determines whether you want to stay with that job or move on and find another employer, or even try your hand at freelancing.

A number of different things can affect your overall satisfaction, and I'll cover all of them here. Then, I'll explain why branding is important to help you find a job that hits on all of these points.

- Meaning
- Control
- Challenge
- Relationships in the Workplace
- Control over Schedule
- Opportunities
- Salary and Benefits

Meaning

What do you do? Do you feel it is important? Those who aren't doing meaningful work, or who can't get behind their company's mission statement will find that they generally do not put their all into the work they are doing.

It is very important for someone to be happy with the job he or she is doing and to feel as though they are making a difference in some way. This does not mean everyone needs to have a job where someone feels as though he or she is saving the world. It simply means you need to have a job that makes you feel as though you've made a difference, even if it might be a small difference.

Control

How much control do you have in the workplace? Do you have any authority to make decisions or to act as a leader? People do not like being in jobs where they have no say and no control. If you've been in a job such as this – as most of us have – then you know how it feels to be in a place that does not utilize your skills fully.

Many service industry jobs fall into this category, and lack of control is one of the reasons that people do not generally like to stay in these jobs very long. To have a truly satisfying job, you want to have at least some control there.

Challenge

Is your job challenging? There is only a fine line between challenging and stressful. You want to have a job that will allow you to have the ability to use your full skill set to solve problems, but you do not want things to become so stressful that it takes away from the overall satisfaction of the work.

You also want for others in the company – peers and supervisors – to see and appreciate the work you are doing and to acknowledge the contributions you are making.

Relationships in the Workplace

One of the key factors in determining how a person feels about his or her jobs is the people with whom they interact. If they are working in an environment where they can work as a part of a great team, they are generally going to be much happier. They want to like the people they work with – from peers to supervisors. Working with authentic people and cultivating relationships can make a huge difference when it comes to workplace satisfaction.

Think about this for a moment. Just how much time do you spend at work? Generally, you are at your place of employment for at least forty hours a week. Being around people you respect and genuinely like will be much better than being around people who make you feel uncomfortable.

You can be yourself and you will feel more comfortable and confident when you work together and voice your ideas. This leads to better idea generation and a much happier work environment overall.

Control Over Schedule

Do you have any control over your schedule? Are you able to take vacations when you want? If you are ill and need to take time off to recover or go to the doctor, are you able to do it without fear of retribution?

Does the company offer a flexible schedule? Some companies allow employees to work four days a week. Instead of eight-hour days, they put in ten-hour days. This often makes people happier knowing they are getting three-day weekends each week.

When you have at least some control over your schedule, you are generally going to be much happier. This doesn't mean you should demand to be in control of when you work though! After all, the managers need to make sure they are able to cover all of the necessary areas. They have the ultimate say in the schedule of most jobs, but people appreciate those companies that give them at least a little input.

Opportunities

Are you in a dead end job? What type of advancement is there in the job? If you can't expect to keep advancing in the job, it means you will eventually hit a wall. Does the company offer any type of career help, such as additional training or education that can help you to advance? Do they have mentoring and coaching opportunities? If the job does not have any opportunities for you beyond collecting a paycheck, you will generally find that your overall satisfaction with the job will diminish over time.

Salary and Benefits

Of course, this is one of the biggies when it comes to your job satisfaction, which is why I saved it for last. While it might not be the only reason, and perhaps it is not the most important reason, the benefits and wages are generally two of the first things that people think about when they are looking at what a job offers.

The cost of living is rising, and you need to be in a job that considers that, and that offers a salary that reflects the reality of prices in today's world. How much does the job pay? What types of benefits does it offer?

If you can't get the pay you need to live from your current job, you need to make a change soon! This element of job dissatisfaction is often the thing that can cause people to take action and find a new job.

Making Sense of These Factors

The above factors are all important, but they can vary in level of importance based on what you want and need from your job. People who are in different phases of their career may have different priorities.

For example, someone who is in her twenties might have different goals and different requirements for job satisfaction from someone in her forties. Someone who is raising a family may have different goals from someone who is single and wants to remain that way.

Your Satisfaction

When you are trying to determine what job is right for you, take all of the above into consideration and rank them in importance. This will let you know if you are choosing the right job for your current needs and desires. It is a good idea to revisit this list every year or two and reevaluate.

As things in your life change, your priorities and requirements for job satisfaction change along with it. By keeping this list in mind and reevaluating, you can be sure you are always in the best job. If not, you will know that you need to start looking for another one!

What These Things Have to Do with Your Brand?

I haven't forgotten about personal branding! Your personal brand will connect all of the above. All of the factors that are changing this career paradigm from the traditional to the bold help you understand just how you need to change and tweak your personal brand to find those jobs.

Job searches are no longer simple. Life is no longer simple either. Everything is about self-promotion whether you are looking for a new job or you are trying to build your own business.

When you can connect your brand to their business in some way, and show the companies what they need to see about you as an employee, it can improve your chance of getting a job that provides high marks in all seven of those job satisfaction areas.

Follow Your Passion and Your Purpose

When you are branding, you can't fake it. If you aren't passionate about the brand you are trying to develop, if it is disingenuous in any way, chances are high it will not work for you. You really do need to follow your passions in order to come through honestly with your personal branding. Find your purpose and define your identity, then developing your personal brand will be far simpler.

What is Your Passion?

Knowing your passion is one of the most important parts of personal branding, and I can't stress this enough. Many of the other elements in branding will tie into your passion. Without it, you can't build much of a brand at all.

Finding the things that you are passionate about and that you love might seem difficult at first, but it is actually quite easy. I always want my clients to go through the process of finding what they are truly passionate about in life. I can help them find it, but I can't do all of the work for them. They need to dig deep within themselves to find the things they care about the most.

Some of the things you will want to consider when trying to locate your passion include:

- The people you love – family, friends, mentors, heroes, etc.
- Places you've gone that you love. This could be a favorite vacation spot or even a place you've never been physically, as long as it inspires you and gives you joy.

  Activities and hobbies you enjoy.

Make sure you look at the other side of the coin as well. Sometimes negative experiences can stir you to take action and to build your passion and platform against those specific types of experiences.

For example, someone who was the victim of bullying as a child may want to take action to help children today who are going through that same torment. The person's passion can become helping victims and educating people about the dangers of bullying.

As you grow and change throughout your life, chances are high that you will find other passions for which you will care deeply. When you start to expand your number of contacts and friends, and start to look outside of your niche, you will likely find other things to enjoy. When you travel, start a new hobby, or do any type of new activity, you are exposing yourself to new things that may very well become a part of your personal brand one day.

Following Your Purpose

Once you identifyyour passion, you have to have direction and purpose. You need to know where you are going and why you are going there. Knowing these things will enhanceyour brand greatly.

You want to align your purpose with your passion. Know what you enjoy, know your skills, and know how you want to change the world or help others, even if it is just your small corner of the world.

When you have a clear vision of your passion and purpose, you will find that it is much easier for you to find your niche and develop your personal branding statement, which we will go over in Chapter 8.

Defining Your Identity

We'll go into much more depth later in the book on developing your identity and brand, but it's a good idea to look at how you can start to define your identity right now. After all, if you don't know where you stand, how will you ever know how to move forward in your life?

The steps are simple, so get out a notebook and get ready to start working on your personal brand.

Who Are You?

It's time that you get to know yourself. Who are you professionally? Who are you on a personal level? You really need to analyze yourself and answer these questions as broadly as possible in the beginning.

What is it that you do in your career? What are your skills and what do you bring to the table? What is it that you want out of your job and out of life in general? Knowing what is important to you can often help to reveal more about who you are.

On a personal level, you need to know who you are too. No one else knows you as well as you do. What are your hobbies? What are your views on different things? What are your favorite shows, books, music, and food?

While these things might seem inconsequential to you, all of them go into making up you as a person, and thus they can all be important for your branding efforts.

All of these things are a part of you. Take the time to write all of them down in your notebook. Create a column for your professional side and personal side, and make sure you leave some space, as you will start to discover many more things about yourself as you go through this book and start to refine the branding message you want to convey to the world.

Who Needs to Know You?

You need to know yourself, but that's just the start. You also need to have other people know who you are. However, the world has billions of people in it. You can't focus on all of those people. You need to focus on those who need to know you.

Depending on your overall goal for personal branding, this will differ. If you are trying to get a job, then you need to make sure your peers, those in charge of hiring, managers, and the like know you and your brand.

If you are a writer trying to get more people to buy and read your books, you need to look at things a bit differently. You need to consider the types of books you are writing – self-help, mystery, science fiction, etc. – and then focus on finding those people who regularly read those books.

In addition, when branding, it is generally a good idea to think outside the box. You don't only have to focus on those readers. Look for tangential connections as well. If your mystery's protagonist happens to be a champion baker, and the mysteries often revolve around the culinary world, you could target people in that world that might actually have an interest in what you are doing too.

You can grow your brand organically and still make sure you are targeting the right group of people.

How Will They Find You?

This is certainly one of the most important parts of branding, and is one of the areas that I will cover exhaustively in the book. While they certainly can still find you offline, most people will find you online. Whether you are looking for a change in your career, or you are simply trying to spread your personal brand to more people for other reasons, the web is the way to go.

Throughout the book, I will explain all of the different methods and tools that you can use to make it easier for people to find you. Some of the options you will need to incorporate include:

- Social media
- Blogging
- Article writing

I will cover all of these in depth, and even show you how to set up your social media accounts and your blog.

Why Should They Care?

You might be able to put your brand in front of people with all of your efforts, but that doesn't mean they really care about you. You have to make them care and you have to make them want whatever it is you are offering.

You can do this by being genuine, for starters. You also need to have a great story that goes along with your brand. When people can connect with you on a personal level, and when they can see whom you are and what you bring to the table, it can make them actually care.

When they care, they are more likely to follow you and feel invested in you, all thanks to your personal brand.

Rampersad's View on Branding

Dr. Hubert Rampersad is a branding specialist and author of "Authentic Personal Branding". He believes, and rightfully so, that branding needs to be authentic in order to work.

He wrote that:

> No vision + no self knowledge + no self-learning + no thinking + no mindset change + no integrity + no happiness + no passion + no sharing + no trust + no love = no authentic personal branding"

When you break that statement down, it's easy to see all of the most important things that need to go into your branding efforts, and if you are missing any one of those ingredients, your branding will fail.

The formula is simple enough to understand and follow. You should be able to look at it and see just where you might be lacking. Make those adjustments and it really can help your branding efforts.

Get to Know the Basic Elements of Personal Branding Now

The development of your brand requires that you understand and utilize certain elements. While we will go over these elements in later sections of the book, I think, it is important to make sure you know what these are right now, so you can start thinking about them.

The following eight elements are essential to the life of your brand, and you must consider all of them when you are developing your brand.

- Your Story
- Your Voice
- Packaging
- Transparency
- Online Platforms
- Self-Marketing
- Partnerships
- Products

Your Story

One of the first things you will want to do when you are building your personal brand is to write your story. Whenever I'm trying to learn about someone, it helps if I have some information and context for that person, and personal stories are a great way to impart this.

You can find these stories on many personal blogs and websites, and they are important in letting people know more about you. They help people understand why you are doing the things you do. They help people to see that you really are an expert in your particular niche.

How did you become who you are? What drove you to become

the person you are? We'll go into detail on how you can create your own authentic branding story in Chapter 9.

Your Voice

Finding your voice is not always easy to do. In fact, many people find it one of the most difficult. They fear being authentic because they do not know what others will think. This can leave their message and their communications, and thus their branding, stilted and sometimes hard to follow!

It doesn't have to be such a struggle though. Three things can make all the difference in the world. All you have to do is be natural, use simple language, and have a unique perspective.

Being Natural

Talk to people in a natural manner, just as you would to one of your friends. You can, and probably should, keep the communications professional, but that does not mean they can't be friendly. This is true no matter who you happen to communicate to. Try to find a common, natural voice for your blogs, posts on social networks, podcasts, in face meetings, and more.

Keep it Simple

You don't need to confuse your message by using big words. I've always tried to keep my communications as nice and simple as possible. It ensures that everyone is always on the same page, and it can help to create more engagement with people.

What Do You Think?

Simply reiterating the things that others say and parroting their words is not enough in today's world. You have your own perspective, and for your brand to be genuine, you have to communicate it that way. Let people know what you think. This is always more

engaging than simply toeing the line. Just make sure that the perspective you offer is genuine to you and your brand.

▊▊ Packaging

If you aren't selling a product, you might wonder what packaging has to do with anything. This doesn't actually mean real
packaging. It's simply the overall look and design, the package, of your brand. Visual communication with your brand is
highly important, and you probably already know that.

Good design really is important today, and you know the saying – you can only make a first impression once. It pays to take
the time to go that extra mile and make sure your design is
perfect.

For your packaging, you need to consider all of the visual aspects of the brand you are creating, including:

- Color scheme
- Logo
- Photos
- Background on blog, site, Twitter, etc.

In addition to having a great visual style, you also need to make
sure that your package is consistent from one platform to another.

What I'm saying here is that if blue and gray are your colors
you are branding with on your website, you need to make sure
you are branding with those same colors on your blog, Twitter,
Instagram, and more.

Uniformity to your brand is important in person as well. From
your business cards to the way you dress, you want to make
sure you are presenting a consistent image. If people know you
from the type of suits you wear, you might not want to do a
speaking engagement in shorts and sandals.

Transparency

People like honesty, even when it might not always present something in a good light. Being honest about things – good and bad – can draw people to you. Honesty is an unfortunate rarity today, butit is highly important for proper branding.

Of course, you have to realize this is a double-edged sword. When you are honest about certain things or positions, it has the potential to alienate a certain percentage of your audience. Most will appreciate that honesty though.

Still, while transparency and honesty are good, there is such a thing as over sharing, and that can be almost as large a mistake as outright lying. Always be careful about the things that you put out there into the digital ether.

Online Platforms

How are you getting your messages and your brand out to the world? You can't simply shout out of your window and expect anyone but your annoyed neighbors to hear you! It is important to develop online platforms that will put you in contact with those who need to know more about your brand.

Know what you want to deliver as well as the overall message you want to get out there, and then start building your online platforms such as blogging, social media, and YouTube. It can sound confusing and intimidating at first, but don't worry; we're going to cover all of this later so you know just what you need to do.

Self-Marketing

As much as you might not like to do it, self-marketing and promotion is important if you want to get the word out about your brand. You can have the best content in the world, but if you don't take the time to promote yourself, no one will ever see it.

How can you market without annoying people? I'll tell you right now that it's a fine line to walk, but it is possible.

Great Content

Instead of inundating your social networks with posts and Tweets about how great you are, you need to make sure you are posting great information and content that is easy for your followers and fans to share. Post links for that content that go to places such as your blog, and make sure the content actually delivers. Once people start to share your content, you should start to see more readers and viewers.

Ads

You could also take out ads to get more eyes on your site. Google Ads can be a good option, but make sure your brand is something that will actually benefit from these types of ads. If you are simply trying to position yourself for a better job, ads will not likely be the way to go for you.

Testimonials

When you use testimonials from customers, readers, clients, former employers, and others, you can let them do the bragging and the promotion for you. This can help to give you more authenticity as well, especially if you have testimonials that come from other experts in your field.

Partnerships

Here is an area where many people actually fail. They never bother to consider partnerships with other brands that could help them to reach more people and thus grow their own brand. Collaborations are great ways to expose your brand to an entirely new audience, and your partner gets the same benefit from exposure to your audience. It's mutually beneficial as long as you do it the right way.

It is important to make sure that any partnership you consider actually works with your brand and can actually help to grow your audience.

Collaboration in Action

A good example of this would be J. A. Konrath, a novelist who is seeing a substantial amount of success on Amazon's Kindle platform. Once a traditionally published author, he embraced the new self-publishing options offered by Kindle and started to do very well.

He worked with other authors, such as Scott Nicholson, Ann Voss Peterson, and Blake Crouch on various novels and stories after he saw his own success. This helped each of the authors to reach new readers and create new fans. Theseauthors continue to do well with their solo efforts, in part due to the greater exposure.

More than Writing

This works quite well with writing, as you can see. However, that's not the only way branding partnerships can work. It can work well for many different fields and industries. You just need to find someone who is similar to you and who is in a similar field.

Products

Having something to offer makes a real difference with branding. It doesn't mean you have to be a celebrity or an author to have a product that helps to spread your personal brand though.

Thanks to technology, you can have many different sorts of "products" available with little or even no out of pocket cost to you. For example, you could consider e-books, online courses, podcasts, and more as a part of your product catalog.

Whatever type of product you have – large or small – it needs to do several things. First, it needs to be something that is genuinely helpful or interesting so people will want it and feel as though it was worth their time and money. Second, the product needs to beconsistent with your brand so that it can help to spread the influence of your brand further.

As you develop your brand throughout the course of this book, you will start to narrow down your ideas of what types of "products" might work well for you. Once you commit, make sure you are creating the best possible product, even if it is a ten-minute podcast a couple of times a month.

If you ever put out less than your best, your audience will recognize that and it could negatively affect your brand.

Your Name and Reputation Are Important

Your reputation is vital to your personal success in life. It allows others to see who you are as well as what you have to offer quickly and easily, and it lets you stand apart from all of the competition as a unique individual who could be a benefit to them.

Amazon founder Jeff Bezos said, "Your brand is what people say about you when you're not in the room", and that's a very good way of looking at branding. Your job is to make sure they are saying good things!

Stand Out with a Brand

A good brand can show employers or possible clients why you are better than the competition and why they should choose you. A strong personal brand can propel you and your career into the stratosphere.

In the next chapter, we will look at all of the wonderful benefits that you can derive from developing a strong and positive personal brand.

Throughout the course of this book, you will learn how to define who you are and how you want others to see you, and you will learn how to use the tools of modern branding to develop and solidify that image that you want.

I will discuss the pros and cons of having professional brand strategists helping you with the branding journey, how to work with social media and measure your branding success, and so much more as we continue our journey through this book.

Do Not Ignore Branding

Whether you are changing careers, starting a job search, starting your own business, or are trying to improve your position, as an author or expert, branding will help you. Ignoring the power of branding is one of the worst things you could do.

Branding does not have to be overly complicated and complex. Anyone who has the desire and the tools can make great strides with their own personal branding efforts. You can use the tips in this book to get a better understanding of what you need to do and you can start to change the world's perception.

Let's see how we can do this without needing to pull out all of your hair! It really is easier than you might think, and I can help to guide you through everything you need to know.

"It's important to build a personal brand because it's the only thing you're going to have. Your reputation online, and in the new business world is pretty much the game, so you've got to be a good person. You can't hide anything, and more importantly, you've got to be out there at some level."

Gary Vaynerchuk,
Author of Crush it!

CHAPTER 2

Ten Vital Benefits Branding Offers

If you are still unsure of whether taking steps to improve your personal branding are important, here are ten of the biggest benefits proper personal branding can bring to your life. You will find these benefits can aid you in your professional life as well as your personal life.

Show Others You are Unique

When you are branding, you can show off who you are and what makes you unique and special. What is it that makes you the right choice? With branding, you can stand out from the crowd in a good way, and that is extremely important in today's world.

You have a substantial amount of competition out there. Others will be trying to brand themselves and market themselves, and you need to do the same. Even though you might have gone to the same schools and have the same experience as the competition, your story is the thing that makes you unique.

Personal branding allows you to tell that story. That's just the beginning of the benefits though.

Control How People View You

Chances are good that you are a nice and normal person. You don't go out and rob banks or commit other crimes. However, we've all done silly things in our past, especially when we were young. In the connected world we live in today, those things can come back to haunt us, even though they might have happened years ago. Information and photos can last online forever.

With personal branding, along with reputation control, you can make sure that the first things potential employers see regarding you is good. Having more control over how people view you is very important in today's world.

You don't want pictures of you doing a keg stand to be the first thing that pops up when the company interviewing you decides to do a Google and social media search! Even though you might not be able to change the past, you can make your present and your future bright enough to ensure your potential employers only see the good that you have to offer. With proper personal branding, you get to choose the pieces of your story you want to tell.

Of course, this means you do have to use some common sense about the things you do in the future. Hardly a day goes by without a story in the press about someone fired from a job for improper conduct or behavior.

Even after you have your job, it's still important to maintain and build on your personal brand.I will get more into that later in the book.

Use the Brand to Create Opportunities

What do you want out of your life and your career? You can actually use your brand to create the right types of opportunities for your future. Your personal branding will create a unique story and path that can attract the type of jobs and connections you want to make.

The brand showcases you and your skills, and that can ensure you are not attracting opportunities that just aren't right for you. This might seem like a small benefit at first, but just think about how much time it you can save. You don't have to waste time with connections that won't work.

It is possible to leverage your brand to focus on the best opportunities that will benefit your life and your career the most.

Builds Your Credibility

Your target audience, whoever they might be, needs to know you are a credible person or a credible source. This is true of anyone, whether you are an author trying to build a larger audience, or you are on the search for a job that can afford you better opportunities.

When you embrace your personal brand and when you "walk the walk", people are more apt to listen to the talk. By taking actions that align with what you want your brand to be, you can unify the picture people have of you. Make sure that you keep the target audience in mind too. If you make promises to them, you had better meet those promises.

Builds Your Confidence

No one comes into this world readily equipped with a strong personal brand. Even those who might be born into money and power still cultivate their own brand.

Think of the Hiltons, the Kennedys, and other families. Even though they may have the money and the prestige, everyone has his or her own brand or story. While they might have an advantage, they still have to think about their branding. Of course, you can also look at the opposite end of the spectrum.

Consider Oprah Winfrey, a woman who has one of the most powerful personal brands in the world today. She did not come from money or wealth, but she was still able to rise to the very top of nearly every industry she's ever entered. Personal branding, along with some talent, helped with this.

Will proper personal branding turn you into Oprah? No, probably not. However, it will give you more confidence. No matter where you might be starting right now, you can change your world and you can change how people think of you.

Gain a Following

Who needs to gain a following? At first blush, you might think that the only people who need an audience would be writers, actors, artists, and the like.

However, a following and a network are very similar, and most people, regardless of the field they might be in, can benefit from having a network of "fans" and people they know who can vouch for them and who like and admire their work.

Increase Your Visibility

When you have a great personal brand, it can help to increase your visibility, which can be especially helpful for writers and similar creative individuals who have projects to sell. However, better visibility can help anyone. With a strong brand, the "good" stuff is at the front of those search engine results, and this increases the visibility of the types of information you want employers to see.

Whether you are trying to gain more clients, more readers,

more followers, or you want to make sure employers have pages full of wonderful search engine results when they look up your name, working on your branding is the way to make that happen.

Do Well in a Down Economy

As the economy has had quite a bit of trouble, companies have started to tighten their belts. This means many companies are hiring fewer people. They are being choosier with the people they bring on board, so they are putting more effort into making sure you are the right candidate.

Proper branding can show you just how well you align with the company as well as their goals.

Again, this can help other people too. If you have products or services you are trying to sell for your personal business, your branding helps you to stand out from the crowd. People want to spend their money on services and products they trust in a down economy.

Great personal branding can help you build more of a rapport with people, and that can make them more willing to buy whatever it is you have to sell.

Garner a Better Salary

How can having a strong personal brand help you to get more pay? When your brand and your story show how much you have to offer, it can give employers the impression that you deserve more if they hope to retain your services.

Good branding fosters confidence in them, and they are willing to pay more to have you on their side rather than working for the competition. While this might not give you a massive salary bump that puts you into the next tax bracket, great branding can actually help you leverage better pay.

Helps You Understand What You Really Want

This is one of the most underappreciated benefits of personal branding, but it really is one of the most important. When you work toward developing your personal brand, you are able to shape and focus on what you want the world to know about you, and you can shape what you want from your career and from your life.

This lets you learn more about what you want and whom you are, which can in turn lead to an even stronger brand.

Keep Looking for Even More Reasons to Start Branding

The preceding benefits from developing your own personal branding strategy are just the beginning. As you grow your brand, you will start to see other benefits emerge. In fact, you should always look for new benefits that branding provides you. As you see more and more benefits,

Even if it seems hard at first, do not give up on your branding efforts. Branding takes time and commitment to work properly, and you will probably not find success overnight. You need to be on top of your branding efforts all the time.

This means you have to reevaluate and change focus if the need arises. However, when you put in the time and the effort, you will always find that the results are well worth the effort that you put into it.

I'm here to show you how to focus your efforts so you can achieve the best benefits personal branding can offer in the shortest time possible.

CHAPTER 3

Step One - Improve Your Personal Brand by Observing Corporate Brands

Your personal brand is very different from a company or corporate brand, isn't it? With a company brand, the goal is to get customers and clients to recognize the company and what they stand for instantly. While a part of corporate branding might be things such as logo and color scheme, that's just the beginning.

When you think about companies such as Disney or McDonald's, you have an image in your mind of that company as well aswhat they do. The name can evoke emotion in you. This is branding in action. Disney is one of those companies that have some of the most powerful branding in the world.

While corporate branding might be different in terms of scope and some of the techniques, the goals are actually quite similar. You want people to associate you with certain qualities and characteristics based on your name and who you are as a person.

You are marketing and advertising yourself with your brand, essentially, and it can be a good idea to watch the way the big companies take care of their corporate branding. Although you do not want to follow everything they do, you can take some pointers from them.

Let's look at how some of the more successful companies out there are ensuring the strength and durability of their brand from a corporate perspective, and how you can do the same thing with your personal branding efforts.

Showcasing the Unique Selling Point

All companies need to make sure their potential customers know exactly what it is that helps to separate their company's products from all of the other products out there. Perhaps they have higher quality materials or faster service. Whatever it is that helps to make them different from their competitors, you can be sure they will focus on that in their branding.

When you are building a personal brand, you want to do something similar. You need to show people what it is that makes you different, and therefore better than, your competition.

Whether you are competing against other people trying to get the same job, or you are competing against other artists vying for the same customers, you need to show people your best qualities as well as what makes you stand out from the crowd.

Making a Good Impression

Many of the things that a corporation does, from the look of their website and logo to their advertisements, are all in service to their brand. These things help to create an impression. In addition, the way those companies interact with their customers helps to leave a lasting impression.

Companies that have great customer service, such as Amazon, use that to help make an impression. Think of some of the top brands that you actually use. All of those brands leave an impression, good or bad, on your mind. You can do the same, albeit on a different scale.

You want to make good and strong impressions when it comes to your personal brand as well. This means you need to take pride in the things you do and align your communications through social media, email, blog posts, blog comments, and more with what you want your personal brand to be. This will leave people with an impression of you that reflects your brand.

Thanks to the digital world, this is easier than you might think. Whenever you interact with a forum, a post, Twitter, FB, your blog, or any of the other countless options out there, you are leaving a digital fingerprint of being there.

In fact, you are leaving your actual name! Together, these things can combine to help people to form their overall impression of you. We will get more into making an impression online later in the book.

Corporations Watch the Competition

Large businesses that want to succeed need to know what the competition is doing and how the competitors are working their own branding. They want to know what type of products and service their competition is offering. By knowing the competition, they can tailor their own business to make it a stronger competitor. It helps them to know what makes their own brand so special too.

You can and should do this as well. You can use your competition to make your own brand stronger, just like the large companies do. Look at what your competitors are offering and how they are developing and positioning themselves and their personal brand. Build on those things that you learn from the competitors to see how they might be able to help your own brand.

Here's an example. If you are a photographer, look to see what some of your competitors are doing to market themselves and how they are building their websites and galleries. Look at a number of different sites and see which ones are the most effective. Take the things you learn and incorporate them into your own efforts and match it to the brand you are trying to build and project.

A Closer Look at Great Examples of Branding Today

The most successful of brands are following pursuits they love and that they are good at, and they have a vision of the things they want to accomplish. The actions that they take with branding and beyond help them to achieve those goals they have for their company.

These three things – passion, vision, and forward drive – are common in all successful brands today. This is true whether we're talking about corporations and businesses or we're talking about personal brands.

Here, we'll look abit closer at some very successful brands you might've heard of. Learn more about these brands and see just how you might be able to emulate some of the things they've done so you can achieve as much as they have.

Four Brands to Watch and Learn From

The following are five brands, most of which you've probably heard of thanks to the power of their branding. I chose these specific brands because they are recognizable and because they really do a great job at every level of their branding, particularly their story.

I'll touch on each of these companies briefly in this section, but I encourage you to go to each of their sites on your own, just so you can learn a bit more about how they put everything together. Even if you aren't branding in order to start your own business, knowing just how these companies brand themselves can be very helpful and enlightening for you.

Saddleback Leather www.saddlebackleather.com

If you know anything about leather, then chances are very good that you've heard of Saddleback Leather. They are one of the top brands in the area of leather bags, but they are more than merely a retailer. When you visit their site, you can immediately see the personality that went into creating the site and how it helps to accentuate their brand.

They have their own company story on the site, and they have stories from all around the world that help to engage people. Whether it is bullfighting, travel, or any of the other stories and the content on the site, the stories all have a few things in common. They are fun and interesting, and they get the readers to want to know more. It brings them closer to the brand overall and it makes them feel as though they are a part of the story.

Dominos www.dominos.com

You know Dominos, even if you don't eat the pizza. They are the company that's been offering fast and hot pizza delivered right to your door in less than an hour. They've built their reputation and their brand on that promise. On those occasions when they can't deliver in that timeframe, they don't charge for the pizza. This helps them to keep their reputation good and to keep their brand growing.

You can learn a good lesson from Dominos. When you make a promise, always do your best to deliver. It can do wonderful things for your brand. If you aren't able to keep that promise, make it right by treating clients, customers, and others with the respect they deserve.

TOMS Shoes www.toms.com

TOMS are a highly popular brand of footwear that comes in a variety of styles for men and women, boys and girls. The shoes have a nice and unique appearance, and they are all comfortable and relatively inexpensive. Those are all of the things that you would expect from a standard shoe company today. Of course, having a great product is not going to provide a company with the attention it needs to do well in business.

TOMS knew this and they needed to find a way to stand out from the crowd, while growing their brand, following their passion, and making a real difference in the world. The company did something that was truly different and inspiring.

They decided that every time someone purchases a pair of shoes from their company, they would give a pair of shoes to a child in need.

This shows that they care about their customers, as well as those who are less fortunate. It shows the heart the company has, and it even makes their customers feel good about buying shoes from them. All of the work they do for the needy help to showcase just how much they really do care when it comes to people who are in need, and that is really helping spread the word of their brand.

When I first heard of TOMS, I didn't know anything about what they sold. Someone asked me if I'd heard about the company that was giving away shoes to children who were less fortunate. That was the story hook, and it's that way for many people who fall in love with the brand.

Nerd Fitness www.nerdfitness.com

Another brand that's been growing lately is Nerd Fitness. With the plethora of sites dedicated to fitness that are out there today, it can be very difficult to stand out from the crowd. This company knew that going in, but they weren't worried. By finding their niche and developing it, they knew they could find an audience.

They branded with a target audience in mind. They wanted to find the self-professed nerds out there and help those who needed to get into better shape. Their site features inspiring stories, resources, a blog, apparel, and much more. The site does a wonderful job of marrying nerd culture and fitness culture.

The company is more than just a fitness site; they are a gathering place where people can come and learn how to change their lives for the better.

You Can See the Results

With the companies mentioned above, it's easy to see how they incorporate the various elements of branding so seamlessly into their company persona. When you learn about those companies, you might wonder just how that applies to personal branding at first. It actually makes quite a bit of sense though.

As you read through more of this book, you will find that many of the same elements that go into corporate branding will also apply to personal branding. By watching the above brands, and other successful brands, you will be able to pick apart just how they are able to brand so efficiently.

When you can do that, you will find that it is much easier to start incorporating those methods into your own brand.

Measure Your Success Like the Large Companies Do

Large companies always need to know how well they are doing and how successful they are with their branding, marketing, sales, and more. They need to know the return on their branding investment, and this is something you can do as well.

In fact, it is often easier to do with personal branding than it is in a larger corporate setting, simply because you will have fewer moving pieces to consider.

While it can be difficult to measure your success with social media since tracking the metrics can be hit or miss, you do know how many followers or fans you have on the various sites, and you know the types of interactions you have with those followers on the sites.

Check to see if people are sharing or re-tweeting your content. This is a decent indicator of how branding and marketing is going. People do not generally share content they do not feel is worthwhile or trustworthy.

Keep Learning

Keep watching those larger companies and learn from the good and the bad that those businesses are doing with their branding. Adopt and adapt those things that work to your personal branding efforts, and avoid the ones that could sink you.

Throughout the book, I will show you the tools and the elements you need for successful branding, so don't think you are alone in this journey. I will make it as easy as possible. You will learn the best methods of getting everything in your life set up just right so you can become a true branding powerhouse.

> *"Absorb what is useful, reject what is useless, add what is specifically your own"*
>
> Bruce Lee

CHAPTER 4

Personal Stories of Success

Before we get too deep into the nuts and bolts of how you can build your personal brand with the right tools and techniques, it is time to take a moment to step back and examine some success stories from personal branding.

When you look at people from a number of different professions who utilize branding to their success, it becomes clear that branding the right way really can help to boost your chances of success. Seeing those stories can serve as an inspiration to you. You can see the sort of things others have done, and you can follow suit with your own branding journey.

Roger J. Hamilton

Roger Hamilton, creator of the very popular Wealth Dynamics system and one of the most successful entrepreneurs of our day, has a remarkable story. Born in Hong Kong, the author now has the reputation of being the leading wealth consultant in all of Asia. He didn't start out with quite such a reputation though.

Just like you, he had to build his brand and find out just where his passions were in life and in business. He'd always had a great head for business, and a great mind for personal branding though, so it did not take him long to master the art. When he was only 21, he co-founded a company called Footprints. It was a publishing company based in London, England.

Six years later, he developed Hand Technologies with people from Dell. They sold tech from Apple, HP and Microsoft. This was one of the first companies to sell on the Internet. In 1997, he created Free Market Media, and then Expat Living Magazine. One thing is for sure – Hamilton is never one to rest on his laurels. His creation of Wealth Dynamics is certainly proof of that.

What Is Wealth Dynamics?

One of the most impressive creations from Hamilton is Wealth Dynamics. The tool utilizes the concepts of Carl Jung and his work with the I Ching. He divides wealth success strategies into different paths, which you can find in his excellent book Your Life, Your Legacy: An Entrepreneur Guide to Finding Your Flow.

That's Not All

Hamilton also created XL Group, which was a way for social entrepreneurs to connect with one another. The group also takes on various humanitarian projects, such as the Global Volunteer Network. Hamilton also happens to be a member of the Clinton Global Initiative.

All of the things that he's done in his life are part of his passion and his drive towards bigger and better things. His contributions to his peers and other entrepreneurs, as well as to those less fortunate, helped to write the story of his brand.

All of the things he's done have helped him with his brand, and that helps him to find even more success. He's one of the great success stories when it comes to branding and building the life that he wanted, and he can serve as an inspiration to you just as he is to me.

Oprah Winfrey

When it comes to success, and personal branding, few people in the world can match what Oprah Winfrey has been able to do. She has an empire that measures billions of dollars, but it did not happen overnight. She's been working on and building her style and brand for a number of years now, and she's not content to stay in just one field.

She hosted and produced one of the most successful daytime television shows of all time, The Oprah Winfrey Show, and that helped her reach millions of people around the world. She's an award winning actress, a magazine publisher, a writer, supports charitable organizations and now owns her own network and multimedia business OWN - Oprah Winfrey Network. Her book club could make an author a success just because the books carry her stickers on them.

She is one of the most influential women in the world, and no one can argue that the woman knows how to run a business and grow a business. Her personal brand is a huge part of this. Oprah also happens to be one of the few people in the world who can get by with using just a single name. Everyone knows Oprah.

Lady Gaga

The woman wears dresses made from meat to award shows. She always has something unique and different going on with her style and her personal life. Even though someone might never have listened to a Lady Gaga album, there is a good chance that person has probably heard about something Gaga did or said.

Her personal branding style embraces the eccentric, and that's okay. In fact, it is a good idea for someone in her line of work.

She didn't put on the meat dress by mistake, after all! While the music might be different, she's following a similar path (with a unique story naturally) to the one Marilyn Manson, Madonna, and countless others once tread. That's the type of brand she is trying to build because she knows her audience, and she knows what will keep people talking about her.

David Beckham

He's wealthy, handsome with chiseled features and an athlete's body, and comes with a British accent and a soccer ball. Most people in the United States know who David Beckham is, even though most Americans don't know much, if anything, about soccer. The rest of the world knows soccer though, and Beckham was able to turn his skills on the field into endorsement deals off the field all around the world. This helped people in the United States to learn who Beckham was long before he became a transplant in Los Angeles.

He parlayed that fame into endorsements for fashion magazines, spas, clothing, and much more. He is one of the most sought after people in the world when it comes to endorsements today. He's not the only one who used his sports to cultivate a powerful personal brand. You still have the likes of Michael Jordon, Magic Johnson, and Tiger Woods, even post scandal, that have powerful personal brands.

Another star in the field of sports is Peyton Manning. Although most people have never met Manning, they will likely say that he's funny and seems like a fun guy. Again, this is due to branding, the commercials and endorsement deals he takes, and the face he puts forward to the public.

Steve Jobs

Steve Jobs was a CEO who developed and mastered his personal brand early. He understood his company, Apple, and the branding approach it was taking, and he followed suit. Apple products are sleek, simple, intelligent, and easy to use.

Whenever Jobs would present information on new products to the media and the public, you would see him wear the same thing. His outfit was a mock turtleneck, nice jeans, his trademark glasses and neatly trimmed beard. He always presented things simply and with the perfect level of excitement – not too much, not too little – to get people excited about what he and Apple were coming up with next.

People knew exactly what they were getting with Apple, and they knew what they were getting when Jobs would speak. He is one of the few who really melded his brand and his company's brand perfectly.

Donald Trump

Donald Trump is a name that most people in America – and around the world – know today. He's a real estate mogul, an investor, an author, a television personality, and one of the most successful businessmen in the world.

His brand is certainly an interesting one to dissect. While many people who are in the public eye are very cautious of the things they say and the things they do in the public eye, Trump has always been one to speak his mind. Even though you might not agree with the things he say, one can respect the fact that he has the gumption to say them and stick to his guns.

At first blush, you might think this would fly in the face of branding. He's not always "nice", and he can come across as a bit acerbic at times. The thing is that is his brand. He will not mince words. It's served him well in business, and it served him well in his personal life and with his brand. He's honest and open when it comes to his personality.

He's seen success in many different areas he's entered, so it is obvious that his branding style works.

Another famous personality who has a brand that can be similarly barbed is Simon Cowell, the former judge on American Idol and current judge on X-Factor. Despite the roughness of personality he remains as popular as Trump. It seems that transparency in the brand counts for quite a bit in the public eye.

Tim Ferriss

You probably know the name Tim Ferriss. If you don't, then you are probably at least familiar with his book The 4-Hour Workweek in 2007. This highly popular book hit number one on The New York Times bestseller list as well as number one on the lists for BusinessWeek and The Wall Street Journal. He released two other books to great reviews and top spots on bestseller lists as well – The 4-Hour Body in 2010, and The 4-Hour Chef in 2012.

The entrepreneur and author began in 2001 when he founded a company called BrainQUICKEN. The company sold nutritional supplements online. The supplements promised they could help to improve short-term memory and reaction speed in as little as an hour after taking it. The company was successful, and he sold it in 2010 to a private equity firm in London.

Ferriss has also been an "angle investor" for a number of start-ups. He's investing in some companies you probably know quite well, including:

- Facebook
- Twitter
- StumbleUpon
- DailyBurn
- Shopify
- Evernote

Selling the Book

Ferriss did not see immediate success when he tried to find a publisher for his book, even though he was already a success in other fields. In fact, he had collected twenty-five rejections from publishers before Random House bought the book and released it through their Crown imprint. This should be a shining example of how dedication to something you believe in can really pay off.

Of course, once the publisher released the book, Ferriss knew that it might not be easy to get it to sell since he was still an unknown at the time. He cultivated great relationships with book bloggers though, and they were able to help him get out the word on his book.

In addition to help from book bloggers, Ferris had started his own blog. He started this blog about two months before the release of his book, and he still keeps the blog current. His blogging brought people interested in his writing and his theories to his site, and it brought other entrepreneurs to the site as well. Today, the blog remains highly popular.

As you can see, his dedication and persistence really paid off. You should be able to see by now that success is something you have to work for, and it won't happen overnight. By building your brand and increasing awareness of you and your product though, you can start to see success.

Just look at what others have said about Ferriss:

- Wired called him the "Greatest Self-Promoter of All Time"
- Fast Company named him one of the "Most Innovative Businesspeople of 2007
- In 2012, Newsweek proclaimed that Ferriss was the 7th most powerful Internet personality

Ferriss does whatever it takes to find success, and so can you. All it takes is dedication, drive, a goal, and the right tools to help you get the job done.

Lessons to Take Away from the Celebrities

When you look at the celebrities profiled in this chapter, you can see that each of them is vastly different from the others.

I chose these celebrities that have such great, and varied branding purposefully in an effort to show you that no matter what you want to portray with your personal brand, from the "high class" to the "out there", you can do it.

You just have to be true to you and the brand you build.

Here are a few tips:

- Know your audience and play to their expectations with your brand.
- Develop a signature style, as Jobs and Gaga did, and stick with it – you don't have to wear meat and you do not have to stock up on turtlenecks, but you do want to be unique.
- Venture into different areas that interest you and that can work with your brand, just like Oprah, Beckham, and so many other successful people have done.
- Know when to walk away and know when to run. Sometimes, an opportunity will present itself that just won't be right for you or your brand. In those cases, it's best to walk away and avoid it rather than doing it and regretting it later.
- Simple does not have to be boring. You can start with a simple message with your personal branding, and that's fine. Again, just make sure you know what you want and know the people you are trying to attract.

Erik's Story

The value of personal branding has been a big issue in my life. I studied and subsequently practice Physical Therapy. Five years of my life went in to mastering this craft. Soon after finishing my studies I realised that I did not want to be in this profession. I wanted to be in digital.

This presented a great challenge to me in the way that I present myself to the world. Even though I had successfully built several software products I felt like a fraud if I presented myself to the world as a "entrepreneur with a digital agency".

It became bit of a joke between me and a friend. When we went to networking events he would always listen to hear how I would introduce myself.

Eventually, I made the decision. Every waking moment I spent reading, researching and improving my knowledge of my "new" craft. I had enough knowledge, and I wanted to prove it to myself and the world. The way I presented myself to the world was my decision. I had control.

I revamped my social media profiles to portray a more professional look. Updated my bio, profile pictures and paid attention to the content I was publishing.

The biggest part of my strategy was to start a blog where I could write on topics I was familiar with. Blogging is hard and requires dedication. There are times when I am great at it and times where I really suck but the doors it has opened has been great.

It has helped me establish myself as someone interested in helping other entrepreneurs. It has helped me become more established in the digital world.

In this new age, you are your brand. You get to choose how you portray yourself but stay true to who you are.

- Erik Kruger,

Founder – DrillAnalytics, Blogger at DearEntrepreneur

> **" Your brand is what people say about you when you're not in the room "**
>
> Jeff Bezos,
> Founder of
> Amazon

CHAPTER 5

Step Two - Know the Image You Want to Project

How do you want the world to see you? Why is that the best option for you? It is important that you can answer these questions before you start trying to define your brand and putting it out there for the world to see.

No two branding styles will be identical, and that's a good thing. You can stand apart from everyone else. However, you have to know how you want to stand apart from the crowd when deciding what image you want to project. You have to consider a number of different factors, which together help to make up the overall brand and image.

What Are You Trying to Do?

Why are you building your brand in the first place? What is it you are trying to accomplish? Do you want to sell books or are you an up and coming musician? Are you trying to polish your public image to help you land a great job with an advertising firm or literary agency? As you can imagine, the actual brand you cultivate depends on why you are building your personal brand in the first place. You need to tailor your branding to what you need.

By first understanding your goals, you will find that it is much easier to adapt the personal branding blueprint later in the book to your goals and needs.

Regardless of your overarching goals, you have to do three different things if you want to succeed with your branding.

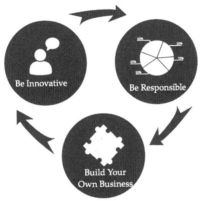

We'll go deeper into each of these areas right now so you have a better and full understanding of what they mean and how to employ the items in your own brand strategy.

Be Innovative

Innovation has the potential to drive your brand and your business to greater heights. It can help you to differentiate yourself from others who are in a similar field, and it ties in quite neatly with the concept of being unique.

Innovation in your brand can help to broaden your platforms and provide you with more success. By visualizing your future goals and what you want your brand to be a few years down the line, you can often develop new ways of reaching those goals. Always keep your eyes open for new ways to innovate and make your brand and your company better.

There are no bad initial ideas. Just make sure you take and dissect all of those ideas to make sure they have the potential to live up to what you need. Change the way you think and definitely think outside of the box with your branding.

Look at all of the various success stories of people out there, and you will see that all of them were "out of the box" thinkers who were willing to innovate and make changes so they could reach their overarching goal.

Be Responsible

When you are building your brand, you also need to be responsible. You have your core values, which we will discuss later, along with your personal branding statement. You need to be responsible to your brand, and that means you can't neglect your brand identity, and you certainly can't go against the values your brand represents.

This is where a number of people actually fail with their brand. They did not spend enough time and energy cultivating exactly what it was they wanted their brand to represent. They don't even know their values, and this makes it difficult to come up with a branding message they can get behind.

Always be looking for ways that you can improve your brand image and make your brand stronger and more cohesive. Actually ask people for feedback and take the constructive feedback and learn how you can incorporate it and improve your personal branding.

If you aren't responsible, you will lose your customer's trust, and regaining that trust can be almost impossible. I urge you to always take responsibility for what you do, as it really is ultimately in your own best interest.

Build Your Own Company

You are different from everyone else on this planet. You are different from everyone who has come before you and everyone who will come after you. This is your strength. Your uniqueness means that you have the potential to build a brand, a reputation, and a company that is entirely yours. Whatever it is you might want, you will be able to build it when you put in the work and have the right tools on your side.

As you build and grow, keep on learning and adapting to the changing world. Find the best ways to bring your unique vision to life and to present your story to the rest of the world.

Define Your Values

Your values can and should be a very important part of your personal brand. Having a set of values you define and live by can help you make the right decisions for your branding no matter what choices you have to make. These values are the principles by which you live, and by which people will view your brand. Again, keep in mind that your values might differ from those of others, and only you can define values for yourself.

Your values need to align with your brand, your work, and your life in order for you to be happy. Defining your values is useful for more than just building your personal brand. It is about understanding and bettering the type of person you are.

How Do You Determine Your Values?

Most people have a decent understanding of their values, but they don't always know how to express what they might be. While you may have a number of different values by which you generally live, you will find that some of these are more important to you than the others. You want to know what your core values, the principles you will never abandon, are.

You can find out what they are by listing ten to twenty of these values that come to mind. Then, narrow your selection until you have just three that are the most important to you and what you stand for. They will be your three core values.

Of course, in this case, three is just an arbitrary, but good, number. You could have more or fewer values that you incorporate into your personal brand. Make sure the ones that you choose to focus on for your brand are really the ones that align most closely with it and with the image that you want to project.

At this stage of brand building, take your time and sort through some of the most common values to see what really works for you. You could re-brand later if you need to, but putting in a bit more effort now and choosing wisely from the beginning is a far better idea.

Explore Various Values and Choose What Works for You

What are some of the universal values people today hold? The following is a short list that covers just a few ideas to help you get started. Use the ideas on this list and come up with some of your own too.

After all, only you can determine what values you hold dear and want to project with your personal brand.

List of Values

- Abundance
- Affluence
- Acceptance
- Appreciation
- Accomplishment
- Balance
- Accuracy
- Beauty
- Adaptability
- Boldness
- Adventure
- Brilliance

- Challenge
- Charm
- Comfort
- Commitment
- Completion
- Concentration
- Connection
- Consistency
- Control
- Courage
- Creativity
- Diligence
- Discovery
- Diversity
- Education
- Elegance
- Enjoyment
- Experience
- Fairness
- Family
- Fitness

- Focus
- Health
- Honesty
- Integrity
- Intelligence
- Joy
- Justice
- Learning
- Pleasure
- Privacy
- Professionalism
- Recreation
- Resilience
- Restraint
- Simplicity
- Sincerity
- Spontaneity
- Stability
- Strength
- Trustworthiness

These are just a handful of different values that you might find important. You can be sure that others, such as employers or customers, will find them valuable as well. It might seem as though all of the values on this list are important, and they are. However, they may be important to different degrees for different people. For example, for one person, family might be the most important thing. For another, it might be honesty.

Add to this list and then find out which values are the most important for you and make those a focal point for your personal brand.

When you are choosing what values to project with your personal brand, you should also consider your target audience as well as what they consider important. Aligning your values with the values of your target audience, as long as you are sincere, can make quite a difference in how well people connect with you.

Of course, you don't want to change your values just to land a job or to sell more. Compromising your values and adopting ones you do not believe in is a sure way to failure and unhappiness.

Ask for Help

When you are trying to come up with your image, you do not have to rely solely on yourself. Instead, you can ask your friends and family to help you. Since they are the people who know you the best, they can often illuminate some of your best qualities, traits, and values, including those you might not even realize you possess.

Ask people close to you for honest feedback and listen to them, even if what they have to say may seem a bit harsh. People rarely see themselves as they truly are. You might not notice some of your best qualities. However, this also means you might not notice some of your faults either.

Having someone you trust and that cares about you helping you with this process can be extremely helpful. Just make sure you do not become overly sensitive or retaliatory when they mention some of the things you might want to work on changing.

Knowing how other people see you is important in branding. You can learn what they see and you can tailor your image to what you want to project. By doing as much tweaking and planning as you can in the early stages, it can relieve you from quite a bit of rebranding later.

What Do You Enjoy? What are Your Strengths?

Where do your interests lie? What types of things do you like doing? Try to align the things you enjoy with your brand and your goals. When you are able to line everything up like this, you can infuse the passion you have for your interests into your brand, and it will really come through. It also helps to ensure you are reaching people who have common interests or goals.

At the same time, you need to know how to play to your strengths. What are you good at doing? Utilize your talents as well as your knowledge and skills you've acquired through life. Play to those things, and do not forget your weaknesses. You need to know your weak areas so you can improve them and so you can turn them to your advantage.

How Are You Unique?

When you are cultivating your image, uniqueness is important, as mentioned earlier. What is it that makes you unique and different from the competition? What makes you special? What is your story?

Your story is what will make you unique in today's world, and it is important to concentrate on developing your story. We will go over this in detail later in the book.

As a part of your personal brand, highlight everything that can help to set you apart from others. If you are applying to a law firm, were you in the military working as a JAG attorney previously? What credentials do you have? What makes you an expert? What is it that makes you special? With so many people clamoring for attention today, you need to find ways to stand out from the rest of the rabble!

Examine the External and the Internal

When you are building your vision and your brand, you need to make sure you are looking externally and internally. Look at the large goals and the small ones too. What is the "big picture" you are trying to accomplish? You can then look at the tools you need and the steps you have to take to reach your goals no matter how simple or lofty they might be.

Once you step back and examine what you offer and who you are, it is much easier to decide what you want to present to others when it comes to your personal brand.

Do the SWOT Test

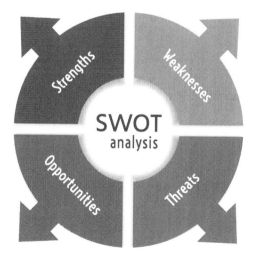

The SWOT test is something that many branding professionals will tell you to do when you are trying to build a unique brand.

SWOT stands for:

- ✅ **Strengths** – What do you have that gives you an advantage over others who might be branding similarly?

- ☑ **Weaknesses** – What might put you at a disadvantage, and how can you make sure this does not happen?
- ☑ **Opportunities** – How can you use your brand to create more advantages unique to you?
- ☑ **Threats** – These things could cause problems with your branding. Know what they are and try to eliminate them, just as you would with weaknesses.

When you keep these four things in mind, it really does help you to develop a brand that resonates with you and the audience you hope to target.

Dealing with Your Weaknesses

When it comes to weaknesses, it is important to know what they are but not to let them define who you are. As mentioned, you want to know your weaknesses so you can shore up those areas. Everyone has areas where he or she might be a bit weak, but that doesn't mean those areas have to stay weak.

Make the Changes and Build Your Brand the Right Way

Only by examining everything you have to offer, as well as the things you lack, will you be able to know where your true personal brand lies. In addition, you need to know what opportunities are available for your branding style and how you can take advantage of them.

When you know what you want and where you need to do, and you know your values, your strengths, and your weaknesses, you are in a much stronger position to start building a great brand that really works.

> **"The more you like yourself, the less you are like anyone else, which makes you unique "** — Walt Disney

CHAPTER 6

Step Three - Who is Your Target?

Who is your target? Whom are you trying to reach? Since there are so many different reasons to build a personal brand, the target will be different for everyone. Some audiences are not right for you, so taking the scattergun approach that many people take with branding and marketing is rarely a good idea.

Instead, learning to target the right group will help you garner much more success. Too many people who are just starting out building their personal brand make the misstep of trying to appeal to everyone.

No matter the goal of your branding, it boils down to the same thing. You are trying to sell something, your services or your product. You have to know the best possible customer type for whatever it is you are trying to sell.

After all, you would not try to sell water to a man who is drowning! However, someone trudging through the desert would probably pay for some water. Know the audience that needs you and you will find success.

Whom Do You Want to Reach?

Who do you imagine to be the ideal audience? What type of client or customer do you want? What type of workplace would be perfect for you? Take some time to write down a few of the things you want from the perfect client or employer. Write down anything that comes to mind and that you feel is important to you.

Perhaps you want to work for a place that actually appreciates you and what you offer. Maybe you are looking for an employer that can offer room for advancement. You could be looking for a company that can give you the pay you feel you deserve. It is also possible that you could be trying to attract a large audience that wants to buy the products you create. This is what celebrities are doing when they build their personal brands, and is a tact anyone can take.

Different Targets

Once you define what you want, it is easier to know where to focus your efforts. If you are trying to get a new and better job, your audience is potential employers. If you are trying to improve your position at the company you are currently working for, your audience would be your peers and superiors. Entrepreneurs are looking for people who will become their customers.

Know your target, and then start your research. We will look at ways you can target each of these different segments.

Looking for Prospective Employers

If you are hunting for a better job or a job in a field you really love, you need to know what you want and align that with employers who are able to offer all, or at least most, of those things. Even if a job pays well, it will not be worthwhile to take it unless you really enjoy what you are doing.

When you are researching and trying to define what the perfect audience will be when it comes to employers, you must consider several things.

Location

Where are you geographically? If you are in Los Angeles, and you want to continue living there, it would not make much sense to start targeting companies in Seattle or New York unless telecommuting is an option. If you aren't ready to pick up and move, make sure you choose companies and employers in your area.

What You Offer, What They Need

These two things really do need to go together if you hope to find a great employer. Know your strengths and the skills you offer, and make sure that the company actually needs someone like you. If you have a specific specialty or niche, you may find that it has both pros and cons. First, you will have a limited number of potential employers. However, it is generally easier for you to find those companies that are hiring for your specialty.

Remember Your Values

Earlier, we went over the importance of values, as well as how you could choose the ones that were the most important to you and your personal brand. Now is one of the times it will come into play. You need to make sure the companies you are considering are in line with your values.

While this can be difficult to ascertain before you actually start working for a company, you may get a good idea of what the company stands for through their own corporate branding. Look at the values they project and make sure they are in line with your own values. If they are not, you might want to eliminate them from your search.

Targeting Customers and Clients

If you are building your personal brand in an effort to find more clients and customers for your personal business, you need to consider similar things to make sure you can be successful and that you are reaching the right people with your message.

Make a list of the characteristics that you feel would make for the ideal customer, client, or follower for you. Once you have a list of traits for the ideal person, it is time to do some research to see where you might be able to find them.

For example, if you are a comic book writer, and you have a comic book on the shelves or for sale online, where do you go to spread awareness of your brand? You have a wide range of options.

In the real world, you can go to comic book conventions, comic book stores, and bookstores.

In the virtual world, you can frequent sites, blogs, and forums dedicated to comics. You can focus your social media efforts, which we will discuss later, toward finding potential readers and customers.

In addition to knowing where you will find them, you want to know as much about them as possible.Research will get you there.

Easy Ways to Research All Your Targets

No matter what type of targets you have in mind, researching them to learn as much as possible about them is very important to your success. Once you have started to identify the ideal targets, it is time to do even more research.

Finding the information you need is easier than ever today. Make sure you keep everything nice and organized, and update it frequently with any changes that might occur. For example, if you've been trying to get work at a specific company, and they have a change in staff, make a note of it.

Using the Web and Offline Methods for Research

The web is a wonderful resource when you use it correctly. However, the web is not the only option you have. Consider all of the different choices you have when it comes to offline methods or researching companies as well as potential customers, clients, and fans.

Finding Employers

You can find a number of great resource sites to help you locate the ideal employer on the web. Use LinkedIn to learn more about the company and the people who work there. Check out local online business journals for your city to learn more about the up and coming businesses and the already prosperous companies.

Check out business resource sites too. Once you find a few companies that might be right for you, check their official websites to learn more about the company and their mission statement, values, etc.

The more research you do the better off you will be when you are trying to pinpoint the perfect place to work. You will also be able to make sure your personal brand is in line with what they want from an employee. This can help you save quite a bit of wasted time and effort.

Some experts feel that attending a trade show or a conference where certain companies will be is a good idea. In fact, it can be a great way to see how those companies act in different settings without them even knowing you are observing them. These shows are not the only thing you should do, but if you get a chance to go, it might be a good idea. You can learn more about the company as well as what they really do.

This could give you a better idea of whether they are right for you and vice versa. You can also get business cards from people at the company and you can get some inside information on what they want, so you can make sure your brand is similar. Later, you can try to connect with them on LinkedIn and other social media sites.

Finding Clients, Followers, and Others

If your goal isn't finding a new job with your personal branding, and you are trying to increase the number of fans or personal clients you have, then your approach to research will be a bit different.

Once you know the type of people who are ideal for your audience, you can use the information you have about them to find out where they are likely to be, both online and offline.

The following are three of the best places to start researching potential customers and fans.

The Competition

Who is your competition and who are your peers? Even though you are trying to build a personal brand, that does not mean you do not have competition and peers. Even though they might not be identical to you, they will be similar, and that means you could have some crossover when it comes to your audience. See what your competition is doing and you will likely find prospective people for your audience.

Blogs and Forums

What would your potential customers and audience read on the web? If you are searching for the right audience that is in line with your developing personal brand, chances are good it will be things similar to what you would read and search for on the web. Look at the blogs they are reading and the forums where they congregate. You never want to push too hard with your brand or any marketing for that matter, but you do want to get your name out there. If they like what they see, they will come to you.

Social Media

If you are running a company, or you are just building a personal brand, you can't get away from the importance of social media. These networking sites are highly popular, and they are everywhere. Make sure you are a part of the top sites, such as Facebook and Twitter, and a member of any specialty sites that might fit in nicely with your niche.

Something to Keep in Mind

When you are branding, you should remember that branding does not mean constantly marketing. While your brand is certainly a huge part of the way you market yourself to the world, it is about showing the world what you have to offer, and why you are someone worth following or hiring.

It is about being a leader, not just a promoter. If the only thing you are doing is promoting, you can be sure employers and others will see through that once they learn more about you. The brand has to be authentic. Otherwise, it just won't work no matter how much effort you put into it, at least not for long.

Fortunately, those who are genuine with their branding do not run into these issues very often.

What Makes Your Target Come to You?

You can target the right crowd, but if your brand is not something that appeals to them, they will not follow you. It is important to try to get on the side of the people you want in your audience. You need to do this on an emotional level as well as on an intellectual level.

The Intellectual Level

The audience needs to know what it is you can offer and what qualities you have that they need or desire. In the case of employers, it can be helpful to have someone who is highly professional and cool under pressure. It might be important to have someone who is creative and who thinks outside of the box.

Your job is to show the audience exactly what you offer so they can see you as a good option.

The Emotional Level

However, appealing to the intellectual needs of the audience is only a part of it. You also have to appeal to them on an emotional level. One of the best ways to do this is by developing a personal story that can go along with your brand.

It is also important to highlight certain features that can make you appear to be a better choice on a human and likable level. For example, loyalty is important to many, and showing your loyalty can generally work in your favor.

Again, your development of your image and your research can tell you exactly what you need to do in order to get the right type of audience. It is not too difficult to do, but it does take some time and some effort.

Developing Your Message

If you want to target the right customers, clients, fans, and followers, you need to make sure you are sending out the right message. With the right message, you can attract the right people. You need a strong and clear message, and you need to be able to let others know what that message is quickly and succinctly. This is very similar to your personal branding statement, but they are not necessarily the same thing.

Of course, telling you that you need to develop your message and not giving you any insight into how to do that is unfair, so I've prepared a few tips that will help you along your way.

It Needs to Be Easily Understood

If you want your message to do its job, it has to be easily understood by everyone who sees it. This will let them know immediately if you or your company has something they want or need. It lets them know whether they want to follow you and learn more about you. The message must be clear and it has to connect with your overall vision of what you want your brand to be.

By knowing the audience you want to capture, you will find that it is often easier to create a message that will actually appeal to that core audience. When you can appeal to your core, you know the message should start to attract others who are similar and who are a part of your target.

It is highly important that you spend enough time researching your target so you know whom it is before you start creating your message. Trust me; it will be much easier if you take that approach.

Make it Memorable

Of course, your message also needs to be memorable and it can't simply be a retread of something another person or another company is doing. Your brand is unique, and your message needs to reflect that. Don't use the first message that you develop without giving it some serious thought. Work on several different messages and take the best parts from each. Spend time creating something that you feel is truly memorable for your message.

Something else you might want to do is crowd source the message in a limited capacity among friends and family. As long as you can trust them to be honest with their assessment, they can let you know whether your message is actually on target or if it needs to have some more work.

Try to Strike the Perfect Balance

As with all areas of branding, you want to have balance. It is important that you create a good and viable message without being overly pushy or abrasive with the message. Persuasiveness without being pushy can be a difficult balance to strike.

Again, play around with your message and see what other people in your life think of it. Also think about how you would feel if you were to be on the receiving end of such a message. If you don't do anything that would make you feel uncomfortable, chances are very good that it won't be perceived as too pushy to others. Remember, you want your message to be friendly and inviting.

Focus on Your Benefits as a Brand

Another important part of developing your overall message, and the feel of your brand, is letting the fans, readers, customers, and others know more about the benefits that you offer and the reasons you are better for them than others in your field.

Your brands should be a part of your message. You want them – at least the most important ones – out front and easy for people to see and understand. Clarity and simplicity, along with your benefits and features, ensure you have a good message for your audience.

I feel it is well worth the time and effort to make sure you develop a message that is unique to you and your brand. When you understand how to target your audience and keep on growing your brand, success really is just around the corner.

Embrace Social Media Fully

Social media can be a boon or a curse. We will go much deeper into social media and its importance later in the book, but I'd like to address one of the biggest issues that I see with social networking and media.

Laziness.

Too many people start building accounts on Twitter, LinkedIn, Facebook, and all of the other sites, but they don't actually keep up with it. Keeping up to date with social media isn't always easy, but you can't ignore it. Too many people are using social media today. Your target audience, whoever they might be, is on social media, and you need to be there too.

Don't fall into the trap of getting lazy on the sites. You need to use them regularly, and you need to interact with people. You also need to make sure that you keep up with any of the new changes to social networking, including popular new social sites.

Technology changes all of the time, and you need to find ways to stay on the same cutting-edge as your target audience. This way, you can keep up with them online and know where they are.

In this book, I'll show you how to set up social networking accounts on all of the major sites so there is no guesswork when you get there. In Chapter 10, I'll explain how to get going with:

- Facebook
- Twitter
- LinkedIn
- Google Plus

I'll even give you plenty of tips on how to post, what to post, and even when to post so you can get the most out of your social networking time.

Know Your Message Goals

You should also make sure you know what the goals are for the message when you are writing it. Knowing your goals will make it easier when you are writing or reworking your message.

How many people do you feel your message needs to reach? Aim towards that target and that number, and if you don't see success at first, don't worry. Messages in personal branding and marketing change quite often, and you certainly won't be the first person who has to tinker with the message you are trying to send.

Make the necessary changes to your message to gear it toward your target. Look at where the last message might have failed and then find ways to make sure your newly targeted message does not meet with the same failure.

Some Parting Tips to Help Your Aim

Here are a few things to keep in mind as you are narrowing your focus and using laser precision to find your audience and to help you when you are in the development stage of your message.

Understand the items in this list, and it is much easier to create a message that is worthwhile and that will speak to your target.

- ✅ Know the target audience you want to have
- ✅ Know your niche or specialty
- ✅ Know your similarities to the crowd and your differences
- ✅ Keep researching to find the best places to locate your audience
- ✅ Reiterate what makes you special and right for them
- ✅ Know what you want the message to do
- ✅ Have an idea of how many people you want the message to reach

> **" If people like you they will listen to you, but if they trust you, they'll do business with you "**
>
> ZigZiglar

CHAPTER 7

Step Four - Know Your Specialty and Own It

Whether you have your own business or not, you should really think of your personal brand as something of a business simply because of the way you need to run it to make sure it is working right. Many experts even call personal branding the "you business", and that's an accurate assessment.

A big part of knowing your specialty will also be identifying and knowing your competition. Knowing the competitors and seeing where and how they specialize can help to give you personal insight into what your niche or specialty should be. Do not make the mistake of doing the same exact things the competition is doing – it will backfire. Instead, look at what they do and adapt it. Look at their specialty and find your own, or find a way to make yours unique from what they are offering.

You need to find the perfect niche and then reach out to your audience from there. Of course, one of the big problems many have when trying to build their brand or expand it is in actually choosing or defining their specialty.

How Do You Define Your Specialty or Niche?

Everyone will have a different specialty, and determining the specialty depends on a number of different factors. In order to help you understand what your niche should be, answer the following questions.

- What is the target market and where are they?
- What can you offer?
- Why are you special and different from others?

Compare your answers with what your competition is doing and see what specialty area you might be able to fill. You want to try to fill a void somehow, or find a way to make you look better to the audience, even if you are in the same specialty as your direct competition.

Become the Master of Your Niche

This is the goal. When you can master your niche, no matter what it might be, people will immediately think of you whenever they think about that niche. You essentially meld your personal brand with the niche so that they go together better than chocolate and peanut butter.

Narrowing the Focus and Honing in on the Right Group

Doing this takes a lot of work, but you can achieve this when you are willing to put in the time and the effort. Instead of using broad strokes to paint your picture of the perfect clients or employers, you are narrowing that focus with razor precision. It can limit the number of potential clients, but when you really own your niche, you can be sure that all of the people inside that niche who need your services will come to you.

The research you do early on to find your target market and audience will let you know if there are enough people in your niche for your needs. You will not usually run into an issue in terms of numbers of people. If you do, you can broaden your focus a bit until you have enough.

How to Make You Special

No matter what your field is, no matter why you are developing your personal brand, people will compare you to your competition. It is inevitable. In fact, you might want to do the same thing. By comparing yourself to others, it can give you more insight into what they offer and what you should be doing differently or similarly.

Here are a few of the things you will want to consider.

- Do the competitors target the same market?
- Is the niche different?
- What do they offer?
- What are they lacking?
- Are you trying to usurp competitors with more influence and experience than you currently have?
- What can you provide?
- Can you narrow your specialty further?

Fight the Fears

When you are putting your personal brand out there, it can be very frightening. Even more than putting your company or your book out in the public, you are putting yourself in the public's eye. This means the public will judge you – good and bad – and that can sometimes be difficult to take.

Fear and trepidation, based on your competition as well as the public, can sometimes overwhelm those who are new to branding and marketing themselves. It is true that you do need a thick skin, and you have to learn that you can't take everything people say – especially people on the Internet – seriously.

You've taken time to develop your specialties and your expertise, and that's more than many people can say. In the face of adversity or the fears you might have, it helps to follow a certain code in order to maintain your balance. Here are some tips to help you with this.

- Be honest – Be as authentic and honest as you can be with your personal brand. Yes, putting yourself out there is scary, but authenticity goes a long way. You will likely have more fans than you will have detractors when you do this, regardless of the reason you are building your personal brand.

- Keep a positive outlook – Even when times are tough, and even when those few people say negative things, keep positive. Most of the people or employers will be pleasant. Focus on them rather than the negativity.

- Don't resort to the same tactics – We've all seen celebrity meltdowns in social media and on blogs. Authors lose their cool with reviewers. Actors go after paparazzi. It's important to keep yourself on the straight and narrow.

- Don't resort to doing the same things that others are doing to you.

- Do what you say you will do – Keep your promises. If you can't keep them for some reason, make sure you let people know why as early as possible. This fosters trust, which is important when building personal connections with your brand.

- Stick to your guns – Just because someone comes along and offers you money or prestige, you don't have to take it. In fact, if this goes against your brand and the image you are trying to cultivate, you should not take it. Doing so would destroy what you've been trying to build. Remember how important your values are. Those same values are important to the people following your brand, and you do not want to lose them.

When It Becomes Too Much

Even though the above advice is all helpful, the pressures of living up to your own personal brand all the time can still feel like an overwhelming amount of pressure. This could be because you are trying to handle too many things.

Sometimes, you just need to take a step back and relax for a little while. Unwind and step away from the brand building for a day or two. Give yourself some time to be you without needing to be the public version of you.

Letting Others Help

All of the work you put into finding your specialty and turning that into your brand is tiring, so time away can be a great way to recharge. You might also want to consider enlisting some help from family, friends, or even professional branding specialists in some cases. They can make things a bit easier on you.

Talking with the Competition

Another thing you might want to do is get some advice from your competitors. This might sound a bit crazy at first, but it can work! Don't contact direct competitors for advice on your specialty, branding, or dealing with the pressures of becoming a public brand. Instead, contact those who are in offshoot specialties, or those who are in the same niche, but in a different geographic location.

For example, if you are an accountant in Idaho and you focus on finding clients in a certain industry you could theoretically connect with an accountant in Florida who does the same thing without being direct competition. Many people, no matter your field, may be willing to help you.

You can consider a number of different ways of finding and contacting indirect competitors. Some good ways to do it include:

- Professional organizations
- Forums online
- Social media outlets
- Websites

Keep Building and Focusing

It may take some time to narrow your field and focus on a particular niche. Going narrower often frightens people because they feel they might not be able to get enough attention in the market to be successful. The world is a big place though, and there should be plenty of success to go around for most specialties.

The thing that will make your take on the niche special is you, and that is why proper branding is so important.

Take some time to think about some of the most successful companies, and individuals out there today. Whether they are actors, writers, or large multinational corporations, each of those brands is special, unique, and has a story to tell that makes it so.

Later, we will discuss more about how you can craft your story to make the most of your brand and the niche you choose.

> **"The key is not to worry about being success-ful, but instead work toward being significant - and the success will naturally follow..."**
>
> Oprah Winfrey

CHAPTER 8

Step Five - Building Blocks of Personal Branding The Branding Blueprint

By now, you should have a good idea of what personal branding entails. You know that the branding has to be an honest reflection of you and your values. The brand is how other people or employers will come to know you, so you need to make sure it is as solid as possible.

In this chapter, we will look at the building blocks of creating your blueprint for branding success. You will have a much better idea of how to put everything together and to launch a successful branding effort.

You need to bring together everything we've discussed when formulating your brand, and you need to see how you can tie all of those things together to create a cohesive personal brand.

What You Need

You can't build a solid foundation and a wonderful house without a plan or the right materials. The same holds true for branding.

The following are the essential materials you need to have and understand when you are building your blueprint. We've touched on these before, but they all bear repeating.

- **Your Needs** – You must understand what you need, want, and expect from building your personal brand

- **Your Values** – These are your principles, as discussed earlier. You should have several core values that help represent your personal brand.

- **Your Interests** – By adding the things that you like and that interest you to your personal brand, you can attract a likeminded audience.

- **Your Mission, Vision and Goals** – What do you want out of life? What do you hope to achieve with the personal brand? Know your goals and your mission so you can construct your brand to reach those goals.

- **SWOT**–Know your strengths and weaknesses, and look for opportunities and look out for threats. Do this as you are building your brand, and after it is in place.

- **Your Personal Attributes** – Know the attributes and personal qualities you have and that you want to show the world and incorporate those into your branding efforts.

- **Your Skills** – These are the things you are bringing to the employer or to your followers. They are your talents, your education, your experience, and all the things that help to make you special.

- **An Audience** – You can't have a successful brand without having an audience. As you learned earlier, you need to know how to target the crowd and make them believe in your brand.

Create Your Personal Branding Statement

Your branding statement is a bit of shorthand that expresses what you offer as well as who you are. You should have your

statement perfected and ready to go long before you start trying to get your brand out there to the world.

You can think of the statement as a very short bio. Some might
want to think of it as an elevator pitch. Here are some tips to
help you when you are creating your branding statement.

- Keep it short. You should have one or two sentences maxi-
  mum in your statement. It should be simple to remember
  and simple to understand for anyone.
- Mention what makes you unique.
- Mention your greatest strengths.
- Mention the value or benefits you offer.
- Mention your audience and the people you can help.

Make sure the statement is consistent with your brand.
It might seem as though this is too much information to include in just one or two sentences, but it is really quite simple
when you break it down. The tagline should make it easy for
readers to know what you offer or what type of business you
are in, and it should be memorable.

Some people may want to add the element of humor to their tagline or statement, and that is fine depending on your brand. If
you are in a field where humor is appropriate, you can include
it. If humor doesn't blend well with what you do though, it's a
good idea to avoid it.

A Good Tip

Keep tweaking your personal mission statement until you are
certain it is as perfect as it can be. A good way to know if the
statement works is to try it on a few people. Read it aloud. Make
sure it rolls off the tongue easily, just in case you ever need to
give an elevator pitch to someone. Ask your friends and family
whether the statement encapsulates everything about you.

Keep in mind that you can also rework your statement later on if you find it isn't working or if you are trying to change your focus. Nothing is set in stone. See what works and toss out what doesn't.

How to Leverage Your Online Expert Status to Become a Published Author or Speaker

As you build your brand and corner your niche, people will start to see you as more of an expert in your particular field, and this can lead to some interesting and lucrative opportunities if you know how to find them.

With your personal branding efforts offline and online, as we will discuss later, you can show people your expertise and the knowledge you have in your chosen area. You will build your platform and your personal brand over time, and you will start to build more trust with your readers and audience through your blogs and through social media.

Once you feel as though you are an expert in your field, it might be time to branch out and grow your brand further. You can do this by becoming an author or a speaker.

Benefits of Being a Speaker

Working as a speaker, in addition to whatever else you are doing with your personal brand, can be very rewarding and beneficial on a number of different levels. Let's examine six of those benefits now.

- **Monetary** – When you speak at engagements, you are not doing it free of charge. Those groups and organizations will pay you to speak and impart your knowledge. You have the potential to make thousands of dollars every time you speak.

✅ **Create New Content** – You can record your speaking engagements and sell the audio and video content. You can turn some of your talks, or part of them, into blog posts and articles as well.

✅ **Rewarding** – When you stand before a crowd of people eager to hear what you have to say and eager to learn from you, it is a great feeling. Knowing that you are making a difference, even if it is a small difference in someone's life, is important.

✅ **Travel** – Some speaking engagements will take you all around the nation and to other parts of the world. Those who enjoy travel will likely enjoy the circuit as long as they have some time to enjoy each destination.

✅ **Boost Brand Recognition** – The more you speak the more people will know you. Your brand will spread, and that means you can attract even greater crowds at your next speaking engagements.

✅ **Develop Relationships** – When you are going to all of these events and speaking, you are meeting potential fans, clients, customers, and peers that can become a part of your network. Networking can be immensely important to furthering the reach and power of your brand.

Tips for Becoming a Speaker

Those who are already celebrities or high profile people usually have little trouble booking speaking engagements. People already want to hear them speak because of who they already are.

However, you don't have to be famous to become a speaker. You simply have to position yourself as an expert in a particular field, and then you have to start by seeking out those speaking engagements in the beginning. Speaking can be a great way to increase your income and to meet new people who could become your clients or customers.

Let People Know

Put information on your website and blog about your availability as a speaker and let organizations know how they can contact you. Consider looking into different conventions and gatherings of people in your field or on the periphery of your field. Contact the people who organize those events and offer your services. You could even hold a class or lecture in your own area if you choose.

Start Small

When you first begin as a speaker, it is generally a good idea to start small and with a crowd that is not too large or intimidating. Even if you consider yourself a good speaker, you should really think about the benefits of starting small and growing your crowds as you become more confident.

It gives you time to practice and to see what does and does not work in front of a live audience. The more you do it the better you will become.

Consider Taking an Improv Class

Do you have trouble getting up before a crowd and speaking in public? If you do, then you are not alone. Many people suffer from this fear, and it can be crippling. Those who have good information and who want to become a speaker can't let the fear take advantage of them though. You can take some steps to improve your skills before you ever step foot in front of your particular audience.

Something you might want to consider is taking an improv or acting class. This helps you to get over your fears of speaking in public, and it can help you learn to think quickly on your feet. Also, these classes can be quite fun and you get to meet new and interesting people.

This bit of advice is one that many give to screenwriters who have to pitch their ideas to producers and studio executives. Since your personal branding statement is essentially a pitch, you can see how this will help you in this area as well.

Should You Become Part of a Speaking Bureau?

As you start to explore the possibility of becoming a speaker, you will come across speaker bureaus. These agencies will help you to get speaking engagements, and they can let you spend your time focusing on other things. They will take a portion of your fee for the service.

Many find that the service is helpful. However, in the connected world of today, it might not be quite as necessary to have a speaking bureau as it was in the past since it is possible to connect with most groups that might hire you with a simple email. You can do much of what a speaking bureau does on your own.

One of the drawbacks of trying to do things on your own though is that you have to spend a lot of time trying to connect with people who may, or may not, want you to speak.

Keep in mind that finding a bureau is something of a Catch-22. They often won't deal with someone unless that person has a bit of real influence in their field. However, getting that level of influence often takes a number of speaking engagements unless you are already a celebrity in your field.

If the idea of a speaking bureau sounds appealing, here are some of the top options right now. You can find the links for these bureaus in the resource section at the end of the book.

- Spotlight Speakers & Entertainment
- AEI Speakers Bureau
- Key Speakers Bureau
- Celebrity Speakers International

- Jostens Speakers Bureau
- CANSPEAK
- National Speakers
- Professional Speakers' Bureau
- National Speakers Bureau
- The Harry Walker Agency
- Premiere Speakers Bureau

This is just a sampling of the many different bureaus out there today. When you are looking for a bureau to help you with your speaking engagements, make sure they are suitable for your specific type of brand.

For example, if you find an agency that generally represents celebrity chefs, they might not be right for you if your area of expertise is in quantum physics. Research the agency, know their reputation, and make sure they are the right choice for your specific brand before you contact them. It will save you – and them – time.

Becoming an Author

Becoming an author is another thing that you might want to consider. Of course, you are already likely writing blog posts and articles for the web, as we will discuss later in the book. However, you might find that it is advantageous to author a book at some point as well.

If you have knowledge or wisdom you want to impart, and you feel there is an audience out there for a book, it might be time to start writing.

What Will Your Book Be?

If you are going to write a book, you need to make sure you

have enough information to warrant one. The book doesn't have to be overly long, but it needs to have information useful to your audience.

Having a book out also gives you that aura of being an expert or authority, and that may just help you if you are trying to land some speaking engagements or new clients.

Your specialty or your personal brand and personality will dictate the type of information in the book, as well as the overall tone it takes. Are you going to take a casual tone with some humor? Will it be professional? Is it somewhere in the middle? Are you writing to be inspiring? Only you, and your editor in some cases, can determine exactly what content goes into your book and what story you want to tell.

When you write your book, you can use your brand and your personal branding statement as a helpful guide when it comes to the tone and direction you want to take with it.

Once you know what you want your book to be, you can start looking at structuring your book and then developing the actual content. While you are doing this, you will want to start thinking about another question though. How do you plan to get your book into the hands of people who want it?

Traditional Publisher or Self-Publishing?

One of the first things to consider is whether you want to go with a traditional publisher or if you want to publish the book on your own. Both have their benefits and their drawbacks, so we will look at each.

Traditional Publishing

With a traditional publishe r, your book will have the strength of a publishing house behind it. In some cases, you may even receive an advance on the book. These advances are rarely huge, but having upfront money for your efforts can be nice.

If the book sells well, you will earn out the advance and start earning royalties.

Some publishers can help with marketing the book as well, but this is becoming much more of a rarity in today's world. Most of the marketing is still up to the author, and that can be costly.

Publishing with a traditional publisher is a no fuss method of getting your work out there. They take care of formatting for paperbacks, as well as getting the books transferred to digital formats. They take care of the covers and all of the accounting as well, and they can ensure your book lands in more bookstores than you can manage on your own. Of course, this does not leave you with full control over the book, and that is one reason some are choosing to go the self-publishing route.

Self-Publishing

When you self publish, you have more control over what happens with the book. You also have more responsibility and work. You are in charge of more than just the writing. You have to make sure the book goes through the editing process, you have to create or commission a professional cover, and you need to get it ready to go on all of the sales channels you want to hit.

You do have the ability to set your price, and you can make sure the book has the exact content you want without interference from a publishing company. In addition, you get to keep more of the money that comes into you. You don't have to pay an agent and the publisher doesn't take a cut since you are the publisher.

Self-publishing is essentially free today too. Thanks to Amazon's Kindle, the Nook, Smashwords and more, you can publish your e-books free to their sites. CreateSpace, which is an Amazon company, lets you create print books free of charge as well. You only pay for the copies that you buy, and you get those at a cheaper rate. If you are speaking as well, you can buy your books and then resell them at your speaking engagements.

Of course, with self-publishing, you are doing everything on your own. You have to wear a number of different hats – author, designer, editor, marketer, etc. Still, many people like this challenge, and it might be right for you.

Keep Your Quality High

One of the things you have to be sure of, whether you are publishing on your own or you plan to submit to a publisher, is to keep the quality as high as possible.

While typos slip into even the best books, do your best to make sure you catch as many as possible. Read the text aloud or use a text-to-speech program and read along with it so you can catch some errors. Sure, some will still slip through, but you can catch the majority of them.

When it comes to the book's content, try to provide as much information to the reader as possible, and do it as simply as you can. If you can use a $2 word instead of a $10 word, do it!

In some types of books, the information will have some repetition from one section to the next. This often happens when you are trying to teach someone how to do something or when you want to impart just how important something is. Some repetition in those types of works is normal. However, you should strive to say it just a bit differently each time, so as not to bore the reader.

Once you finish writing the book, let it sit and gestate for a while. Go back and read it a week or so later, and you may find some places you can tighten it up and make it stronger overall.

Have someone else read it too. You don't want the person you have read it give you glowing praise though. You want the person to read the book objectively and to tell you where you can make it better.

Hire Someone to Help You

What do you do if you aren't much of a writer? If you have trouble stringing together sentences in a cohesive manner, you always have the option of hiring a co-writer or a ghostwriter to help you. For a fee, the ghostwriter will take your concepts and your core idea and turn it into a book for you.

Keep in mind that when working with a ghostwriter, and even a co-writer, your vision might not be identical. Once they write the book for you, read the manuscript and see what is right with it and what you might want to change so that it aligns with your own brand and outlook. Most of the time, it will only take a little bit of tweaking to make it fit your style and brand.

When it comes to self-publishing, you can hire freelancers to take care of all of the different types of tasks that come up. Hire an artist for your cover. Hire a specialist to help with your formatting. Hire an editor and a proofreader to tighten the writing. You can hire people to take care of nearly every different type of task involved with publishing your book.

Don't Be Afraid of Rebranding

Before we end this chapter, let's look at the idea of rebranding again. This can scare many people. They do not like the idea of reworking their brand from the ground up, and they often feel it will take too much work. You do not have to start from the bottom though. When you rebrand, you just make changes here and there that will steer your personal branding message in a new direction. You can start small and subtle with your rebranding efforts if you like.

Of course, you can take the opposite approach and go large. Your rebranding could be an event if you want it to be. Reinventing your brand doesn't have to be scary at all. Instead, look at it as a fun new adventure that will bring you to where you need to be to find the right audience.

"_Be Yourself, Everyone Else is Already Taken_**"**

Oscar Wilde,
Author and
Playwright

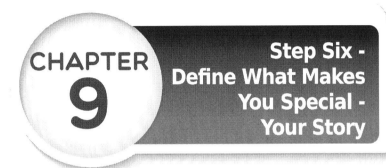

CHAPTER 9

Step Six - Define What Makes You Special - Your Story

What is it that makes you different from all of the other people in the world? How are you unique? If you are an author, you know there are countless others out there like you toiling away over a keyboard working on similar things. If you are an accountant, you know you have hundreds of others, or more, in your own city competing against you. You aren't the only executive, musician, lawyer, or agent in the world. What makes you unique then?

The answer is simple; it is your story.

Your story is different from all of the other people out there. Everyone is a jumble of puzzle pieces that tell a different tale when put together. Your story is what makes you unique and your story is your ultimate strength when it comes to personal branding today.

You Have Control of the Story

It is your story, and you have control over how you tell that story to your audience. You have to be genuine, but you can tailor how you tell the tale to make it fit the other elements of your brand. Your story should be personal, and it should help to connect you on an emotional level with whoever reads it. You are the protagonist, the hero of your own story, so you need a good one.

The rest of your personal branding often relies on the story you tell. A great story means branding will likely be much easier for you. In this chapter, we will go over the basics of creating a good and compelling story that really helps to accentuate your personal brand.

People Love Stories

People have been telling stories since the dawn of time. It is the oldest form of entertainment. People would gather round a fire while the storytellers would weave tales of monsters and magic to help the primitive cultures make more sense of their world. Love of story is something ingrained in us from an early age too. They serve to educate, to entertain, and to make people understand the importance of good values.

Since people are so accustomed to the format of the story, it makes sense to use this as a means of telling others about ourselves. Rather than a dry litany of the things that you have done and seen and the things you believe, you can instead impart that same information in an engaging story.

You will find that people are far more likely to remember the stories you tell than they are to remember a list of facts you spout.

Stories Develop Trust

A good story that is honest and moving can help to develop trust. People want to feel as though they can trust you and your brand, and honest stories can help with that. Different stories, on your site, in articles and interviews, and elsewhere can serve different purposes, and all of them can serve to increase the level of trust the reader feels for your brand.

- ✅ Some of the stories will let people know more about you as well as whom you really are.
- ✅ Some stories show the values you have and how they align with the values of your readers
- ✅ Other stories will show your audience that you understand them and that you understand their needs.

Every Good Story Needs a Plot

Have you ever tried to read a story or watch a movie without a plot? Story simply can't exist without a plot. Something without a plot runs the risk of becoming a series of vignettes or anecdotes that hold little meaning. While they might be fun little tales to tell, they aren't a cohesive story with a beginning, middle, and an end. Remember this when you are creating your own story for branding purposes.

Everyone Knows How to Tell a Story

You know how to tell a story. Kids who are just learning to speak know how to tell stories. Even if you haven't exercised the storytelling muscle in decades, you know how to weave a tale. It might not be Shakespeare, and you might need some practice, but you know the basics of story. You need a beginning, middle, and end to create a story that works.

You can think of the story like stretching a rubber band.

- ✅ In the beginning, the rubber band is in its normal, happy state.
- ✅ Along comes some type of drama that stretches the rubber band and creates tension that nearly reaches the breaking point. This is the middle, where most of the tension should occur.

✅ In the end, the rubber band can return to its natural state. It might be changed, and there might be some fraying around the edges. The rubber band might even be broken. The end can represent change or a return to normalcy. It's all in the type of story you are trying to tell.

Just think about talking with your friends and family. When you come home from work or back from vacation, you tell people stories about what happened. It's human nature.

Let's have a little practice with the following prompts. Tell a personal story with a beginning, middle, and end that applies to each.

✅ What is the most embarrassing thing you've had happen?

✅ What happened on your last vacation?

✅ Tell a story about your favorite pet

✅ Tell a story about something you created

✅ What was the biggest crisis you've handled?

✅ What was the best, or worst, part about high school?

✅ Tell a story about your worst day.

✅ Tell a story about your best day or greatest accomplishment.

These are just a few prompts to help you get going. You can come up with dozens more if you want the practice of putting a quick story together. Whether you write them down or speak them aloud, you should start to see the basic patterns and understand the various beats of the story.

When you start telling these stories, you will naturally have a beginning, middle, and end because you inherently know how to tell stories. The more you practice the better you will become at putting them together too.

How Many Stories Do You Need?

The answer can differ for different people. In the beginning, you might only need to have a single story on your site that lets people know more about you. However, as you grow your brand and start creating online content or speaking, you need to delve deeper and have more stories on which you can rely.

Quick Tips for Building Your Story

Building your brand story should be a fun experience. Taking the time to come up with a great story that has the potential to connect with people emotionally can be thrilling, but it can be difficult. Your first attempt at creating a story might not be perfect, and you might have to work on several drafts to get things right. It's important that you do take the time to do it though. A great story really goes a long way in helping you to create your personal brand, and it is often how others will identify you.

Here are some tips to remember when you are creating your story:

- Be honest above all things.
- Have a full arc to the story – beginning, middle, and end.
- Show don't tell.
- Make sure the story works with your branding goals.
- Show your strengths and how you overcame obstacles and weaknesses.
- Create an emotional connection with the readers.
- Be distinctive with your story – don't ever copy someone else's.
- Your stories are longer than your personal branding statements – they can be a page or more.

Double Down on Honesty

We've mentioned honesty a few times already when it comes to building your personal brand, and it really bears repeating here when it comes to your story. If you are not honest, it will come back to bite you.

Think about just how connected the world is today and how easy it is to find out information about people. If you are dishonest about your credentials, people will know and they will know quickly. It can be hard to bounce back from accusations of being dishonest, and all the work you've done to increase the level of trust your audience has with you will be gone.

Even if you might not think your story is particularly exciting, it is no reason to make up stories. Find different angles and different stories you can use to further your brand instead. It really is in your best interest.

Your Opportunity to Shine

Your story is where you get to shine. It is where you get to be the slayer of dragons and the hero of the realm. As long as you are honest and you understand the structure a story needs to take, you can use your story to help make your personal branding more powerful and farther reaching.

Stories Work for Your Branding Needs No Matter What They Might Be

If you are trying to use your personal brand to gain more exposure and to leverage yourself as an expert, then stories are a great way to do it. However, they can help anyone who is branding for any reason. If you are trying to improve your position at your current company, you can use stories to help you. If you are trying to get a position at a new job, stories that display your talents and skills – without too much bragging – can help. Have those stories on your personal sites, and tell them to interviewers when and where it is appropriate.

Make your stories work for you!

> *"Branding demands commitment; commitment to continual re-invention; striking chords with people to stir their emotions; and commitment to imagination. It is easy to be cynical about such things, much harder to be successful."*
>
> Sir Richard Branson, CEO Virgin

CHAPTER 10

Step Seven - Online and Offline Tips, Tools, and Techniques for Getting Your Personal Brand into the World

With all of the work you are putting into the behind the scenes creation of your brand, you are probably excited about getting it out and into the world. In this chapter, we will cover the things you can do to put your brand into the world online and offline.

Use Both Online and Offline Networking to Improve Both

With today's world being so reliant on communications online, why would you need to consider offline branding and networking? The reasons are simple. Some people who may be a part of your target audience might not be online. You want to reach as many people in your niche as you can find.

You may meet people at a convention or trade show too. Face-to-face meetings, speaking engagements, and the like are great ways to expose more people to your brand offline. Those people who see you can then head online to find out more information about you as well as what you offer.

Melding your online and offline branding efforts can help you to reach out and find far more people than focusing solely in one area could possibly do.

Understand the Basics of SEO

SEO, or Search Engine Optimization, is the method by which you try to increase your visibility in the search engines, such as Google. You want to optimize your site and social networks so you can increase page rank in the search engines.

You've all used a search engine before. When you type in those keywords and the results pages come up, how many pages deep do you go looking for information? Most people will only look on the first page or two for the results they want.

That's why your SEO is so important. You want to make sure your site is within those first pages. The higher your site's ranking the better, and that's just what SEO aims to do.

Tips for Working with SEO

SEO can be quite complex, and it deserves a book of its own. These tips should help you get a decent handle on your SEO though.

- **Monitor Your Rank** – You need to know if the SEO techniques are working, and the only way to do that is by monitoring your standings in the search engines. With Alexa and Google Toolbar, you can see where you stand. Keep track of how many people are coming to your site and where they are coming from as well. Google Analytics can help you with this.

- **You Need Keywords** – You have to have keywords in your content, but you need to make sure you are using keywords that are appropriate for your site and brand. Use the keywords wisely though. Make sure they integrate well within the content so they don't stand out as keyword stuffing, which can cause the search engines to punish your site.It is important to add your keywords to your titles, URLs, and images as well.

✔ **You Need Good Links to Your Site**– Another great way to increase your search engine ranking is by having a number of good external links that lead back to your site. Don't use link-farming sites to get these links though. You want them to come from good and legitimate sites. Linking to your own site from social networks is a good option. Just make sure you do not link excessively and cause the search engine to think you are spamming.In addition, don't link from other blogs or forums unless you are sure it is okay with the site owners.

✔ **Good Content** – One of the most important things for your site, whether you run a blog or a traditional website, is to have excellent content. The content should be interesting to readers, and it should be fresh. Adding new content regularly is a good way to keep the search engines happy.

Keep in mind that the content you add does not necessarily have to be articles and blog posts. You have a number of other things you can use, including photos, videos, and audio. Create the type of content that works the best with your brand. We will discuss what you can do with your blogging in the next section.

✔ **Link to Others** – You want to develop relationships with other sites that might be in a similar field. Link to those sites, and develop your relationship. They will likely link back to you and mention you on their site, which can help you to get more views and traffic on your own site. This will expose your brand to more people than you could do on your own. Of course, when you do this, you want to make sure the linked to site belongs to someone with a good reputation in his or her field.

 Work in the Social Media Networks – Today, social sites, such as Facebook, Twitter, and LinkedIn are more important than ever before. Search engines are now including social media in their results, and that means if you want your personal brand to be a success, you need to make sure you are on all of the biggest social networks, along with any specialty networks and sites specific to your field.

Choose the Best Domain Name

Whether you are choosing a dedicated website as your main presence on the web, or you are choosing to use your blog site for that, it's important that you have your own domain name. You have quite a bit of freedom with your domain name, but that does not mean you can simply choose anything you like.

You need to make sure you choose the very best domain name possible. Here are some tips that will help you come up with the perfect domain. However, keep in mind that the Internet has been around for a while now, and you might not be able to get the first name that you come up with – someone might have already beaten you to it.

That's okay though! Just use these tips and you can develop great domain names that really work for you.

Tip #1 Know Your Brand Name and Tie Them Together

What is the name of your brand? If you are creating a personal brand, it might be something as simple as your name. It might be something else entirely. The name of your domain needs to speak to what you do or who you are.

Take comedian Chris Hardwick's company Nerdist, for example. The company covers and sometimes parodies pop and nerd culture. They have television shows, podcasts, blogs, and more under Hardwick's umbrella. Someone in this position could use their own name for their domain if they are trying to position themselves as the true face of the brand.

They could also choose the name of their company and turn that into the personal brand if they choose. This keeps a bit more distance between the person and the public, and that might be what you want. Either a personal name or a company name could work fine for a domain name.

 ## Don't Be Slavish to Keywords

Some people will tell you that you should use your keywords right in your domain name. In some cases, this might be a good idea, but I would want to avoid it. You are trying to develop an actual brand that people recognize.

Using a keyword, just because you feel it could get the site a high ranking, could be problematic. You want people to look you up rather than keywords that could apply to anyone. When you use just keywords in your domain name, you are actually running the risk of diluting your brand, and that's the last thing you want after all of your hard work of building the brand.

 ## Keep Things Simple

Always keep your domain name as simple as possible. You want it to be easy to say, easy to remember, and easy to type. Even though many people who like your site will simply bookmark it or favorite it in their browser, that's not the way everyone surfs the web. Also, the first time people visit your site there is a chance they will have to type it into their search bar. If they mention your site to their friends, you don't want it to be hard to remember or hard to say.

Be careful with domain names that are puns and plays on words. Even though they might be cute and they might look good on a sign or a business card, people might not know how to spell them and they won't be able to find your site. Don't add numbers to the domain name either.

It might sound strange, but you want the visitor to have to do as little work as possible. Remembering if you have a number spelled out or if you are using the numeral can make things difficult, especially when you are trying to tell others about your site. Don't use hyphens either.

Some people feel that they can use a hyphen and then choose a name that might not otherwise have been available to them since someone else already owned it. The hyphen makes it a new site. Of course, most people aren't going to remember the hyphen when they type it into a search bar, and they will go to the other site rather than yours.

Extensions Are Important

When you start typing in a new website's name that you want to visit, do you do the same thing that I do? Do you usually type in .com without even thinking that the extension could be anything else? I've done this more times than I can count, and I've had trouble finding sites I wanted to visit because of it. Those sites were using other extensions, and I wasn't aware.

While it is great that there are so many different options for extensions today, and it is easier to get the name you want, you do need to think about whether it is a good idea to go with one of those other extensions simply because they are so rare still. Other options include .net, .org, and .TV, but how many people are going to remember that when they are typing in your website?

It's always a good idea to go with .com if you can. If the first domain name you want isn't available, you can always consider some other domain names that might work well for you.

I suggest only going with the other extensions when it is your only choice in the matter. Otherwise, stick with.com.

How Does the Domain Look When Spelled Out?

Sometimes, you might feel you have a wonderful idea for your domain name. It rolls easily off the tongue. It perfectly describes you and your brand succinctly and fully. It's the ideal domain name.

Hold your horses and put your credit card away.

You might not want to buy that domain until you look at some of the following inadvertent naming faux pas that have befallen people all around the World Wide Web.

I've gathered some of the funniest examples from around the web for your enjoyment – and to serve as a warning. You really do have to look at your domain from different angles to make sure it works.

Inadvertently Hilarious Domain Names

- Speedofart.com – do you see Speed of Art or do you see Speedo Fart?
- Choosespain.com – do you see Choose Spain or do you see Chooses Pain?
- ITscrap.com – do you see IT Scrap or do you see its crap?
- Oldmanshaven.com – do you see Old Man's Haven or Old Man Shaven?

These are just some of the mild versions of bad domain names on the web. You can entertain yourself for quite a while when you start to look up all of the other crazy names people bought for their companies without ever realizing they were buying something quite so funny – and wrong – for their domain name.

Moral of the story is to read your domain name out loud and have a few other people you know and trust do the same.

 ## Don't Violate Copyright

You don't generally have to worry too much about copyright with domain names, but you do have to be careful. You wouldn't want to choose a domain name that you know is a copyright someone else owns, especially if you happen to be in the same or a similar business. A good way to make sure you are in the clear is to visit copyright.gov and do a search.

 ## Make Sure the Name Is Available

Once you narrow your choices and you have a handful of domain names that could be perfect, you still aren't done. You have to make sure these names are available before you grow too attached to them.

Some of the best tools for checking the availability of the domain names include:

- Domainsbot.com
- Bustaname.com
- Instantdomainsearch.com

If the name you want is not available, it's not the end of the world. Just go back to the drawing board and think about what it is that make your brand and you unique. You will be able to find a perfect name, and you will realize that it really was worth the sweat you put in to find it!

 ## Shorter Is Usually Better

In addition to being simple, you will find that having a domain name that is short is generally a better idea. You should strive to cut down as many words as possible. The faster people can type it into the search engine and get to your site the better. Shorter is generally easier to remember too.

The preceding eight tips really are very helpful when it comes to developing your domain name. Keep them in mind when you are creating your name, and you will have a name that's short, catchy, and just perfect for your site.

Blogging

If you aren't blogging yet, you are missing a great opportunity to spread your brand and get your message out to the world. Most people, and even companies, have blogs today. A blog is similar to a website, and it has all of the same features you would find in a traditional site. The real difference is the layout and the fact that you can – and should – update frequently with posts.

Blogging is helpful, as it can be a wonderful way to speak directly to your audience on a regular basis.

- ✅ **Plan Your Posts** – So you don't feel overwhelmed when you are trying to write your blogs, it is a good idea to plan them early. You can create a list of topics in advance if you like, and you can write the posts a day or two before you put them up.

- ✅ **Write Timely Posts Too** – In addition to the advanced posts you create, you might have bits of timely news that you want to write about as well. You should add these posts whenever the need arises. This type of newsworthy content can help to bring more people to your blog.

- ✅ **Update Frequently** – Search engines like to have fresh content. This means you should not let your blog sit idle for too long, or you may lose ranking. Once you have your blog schedule, you should do your best to try to stick to it. Try to update at least once a week. You could probably get by with two posts a month, but it really depends on what your audience wants. Many bloggers update at least once a day.

✅ **Edit the Post**–Once you write the post, make sure you edit it for content, spelling, and typos. Mistakes happen, but if you proofread the post, it should reduce your chance of errors. A good trick for editing is to read the post aloud, or have a computer program read it to you. You can find more mistakes this way.

✅ **Consider Mixing Up the Content**–Written blog posts will likely be the bulk of the content on your site, but you should consider branching out with different sorts of content occasionally. Adding photos is often a good choice. Infographics can be a good addition as well. Podcasts and videos are other options that can add more interest to your site. If you feel they can accentuate your brand, consider utilizing them.

✅ **Getting Some Help** – Sometimes, you may not have the time to create your own posts. That happens to most bloggers, especially those who like to update frequently. You can always have guest bloggers, or even hired writers to blog for the site regularly. Make sure they understand your brand and vision though.

✅ **You Must Remember the Brand** – Don't start writing posts that, through the content or tone, go against what you are trying to accomplish with your brand. This is especially true if you are hiring outside help for some of your posts. Here is an extreme example. If you have a blog and brand that tries to espouse the benefits of the vegan lifestyle, you will not want a guest blogger writing about their great pork BBQ over the weekend! Align with your brand.

Setting up the Blog

Setting up a blog today is fast and easy. You can use Word-Press, Blogger, or a similar site and get a blog up and running

STEP SEVEN - ONLINE AND OFFLINE TIPS,
TOOLS, AND TECHNIQUES FOR GETTING YOUR
PERSONAL BRAND INTO THE WORLD

By keeping your audience in mind when you are creating your bio, I promise you will find it much easier when you write your bio.

Utilize Your Story

You've already put all that work into developing your story, so creating your bio is going to be a snap. Take your story, which you will probably have on your site somewhere as well, such as in the ABOUT section, and reread it.

Distill it down to its most basic parts, the most important parts that can tell a reader about you and your brand in a smaller and easily digestible piece. You have the elements you need – you just have to choose which ones to use in your bio. Since it is your bio, you should make sure that you keep the bio solely about you as well, and not on the larger brand.

For example, if you are branding for a jewelry business or soap making business, you will want to make sure the bio is at least 90% to 95% about you and not about your product. The purpose of your bio is to let the reader know more about you and to start to develop more of a rapport with the reader. You give them an insight into who you are and how you came to be that person.

First and Third Person

I suggest that you write your bio in two different ways. Write your bio in the first person "I did this, I did that", and write a version in third person, "John Smith did this, John Smith did that".

Why would you want to have two versions of the same basic bio?

Each of these provides you with a different feel. The first person view feels very close and personal, while the second feels more professional. Depending on the type of blog you are creating, one of these might work better than the other one does for you. However, I feel it is a good idea to have both, and I'll tell you why.

You can try each of them out on your blog and then choose the one that works best. You can use the alternate bio for other things. For example, if you have a book coming out, you will generally need to have a third person bio for the back. If you use your first person bio for your blog, having a third person bio ready to go that is very similar can save you some time. If you find that the bio you posted just doesn't work, try swapping it out with the alternate before you spend time rewriting it.

Once again, knowing your audience will be helpful when you are deciding whether you use first or third person for your blog's bio. If you are building a close and open relationship with the readers of the blog, and most of your posts are in first person, it might actually be a good idea to go with the first person bio. Take the time to figure out what will work for your audience and use that.

What's in a Name?

Your name is important to your brand, and it's certainly important to your bio. You should make sure you have your name front and center in your bio. Always place it in the first sentence and preferably in the beginning. This is very easy to do with both first and third person bios.

Let's see what each might look like for our fictional John Doe.

- First Person – "My name is John Doe, and I've been…"
- Third Person – "John Doe has worked in the field of…."

It's very simple, and that's fine. In fact, aiming for simplicity is always a good idea. Read the bio and if it sounds too awkward or strange in third person, just switch to first person.

Let Them Know the Facts Early

What are the most important things you want your readers to know about you? Once you figure these out, you need to know how you can weave them into the first part of your bio. They should be as near the front of the bio as possible.

Let the readers know the most important things about you in the first part of the bio. What are your most impressive accomplishments? What is it that you bring to the table? If you have done anything interesting and that you feel is worthy – and that matches your brand – add it there. It can serve as a good hook to the reader and make him or her want to continue with the rest of the bio.

Add Some Personality

The bio doesn't have to be static and impersonal, even when you are creating a bio for a professional blog. People are reading the bio because they want to know more about the person behind the blog. A few personal details and a bit of humor sprinkled into the bio is always a good idea. It lets the reader know that you are a unique person with a real personality.

Once again, think about your audience, and make sure that the personality you are injecting into the bio is something your target audience will appreciate. When you add humor, you have to be careful since humor is so subjective. You don't want to run the risk of offending or alienating part of your target audience.

Good to Go... No

Once you write your biography and you think it looks and reads great, you might think you are done with it. Is it ready to go up right now? You need to reread it a couple of times. Read it aloud, and then have at least one or two other people read it as well. You want them to read with an eye toward several different things.

- ✅ Is it representative of you?
- ✅ Does it read well?
- ✅ Are there misspellings?

Even if you are a great writer and you don't have trouble with spelling and grammar, you will run into spelling and grammar issues. It happens to everyone, so always reread and look for errors, as well as places where you can make the language tighter.

Even after you have your bio up on your blog, reread it and tweak it when necessary.

Contact Information

You already have contact information and forms on other areas of your blog, but you want to add it here as well. Always add your email address and other pertinent contact info you want people to have to the end of the bio, or at least include a hyperlink that sends them to the contact form on your site.

Another great idea is to add some links to your social media accounts right after the bio. Even though you will have your social media links elsewhere on the blog, adding them here so people can check out your networking profiles right after reading about you is a good idea. You are fresh in their mind, and they are likely to be

Keep it Updated

New things are happening in your life all of the time. You are doing different things in your career and you are garnering more accomplishments. Your bio needs to reflect this. Whenever you have any large changes in your life, make sure that you add them to the bio immediately.

Do an assessment of your situation every three to six months, and see if you want to change anything else about your bio. This is a good way to keep up with your bio and to make sure everyone who reads about you knows all the latest information.

Photo and/or Logo

Blogs make it very easy to include photos with your text today, and you might find that it is a good idea to have a photo of yourself, or an image of your logo with the bio. This helps to put a face or image to the name.

While most people will want to use a nice headshot, don't feel as though that's the only thing you can do. Choose a nice looking, clear photo that makes sense to your brand. Most of the time – 95% of the time – it will be a picture of you. However, if you have an open and personal style, and you are inviting people to be a part of "your world", you might put up a photo of your pet.

This might fly in the face of what some people might tell you to do with your bio and your blog, but you can find quite a few successful sites that do this. Saddleback Leather owner's Labrador is a major part of their site.

Types of Blogging Styles

When you are blogging with branding purposes in mind, you have to make sure you are creating the right type of posts for your blog. Those who haven't blogged before probably don't even realize there are a number of different styles and types of posts that one can write.

In this section, I'll go over each of these with you so that you may see the different options as well as how you might be able to use them for your brand. Generally, having a good mix of different types of posts will be to your benefit. It can help to keep your readers engaged.

In some of the styles that follow, I will provide examples using an author as the blogger in question. However, I want to make sure you know that these types of blogging are not merely for authors, artists, and the like. You can use these blog archetypes to help you expound upon nearly any type of brand and blog that you are creating and trying to develop.

Something you will want to note is that you should not use just one of these ideas exclusively. You really do need to cycle through them if you want to have a well-respected blog that people actually like to read.

Ambitions and Goals

Another term for this might be goal blogging. In these types of posts, you would write about some goal that you want to accomplish. You blog about your ambitions, and you try to tie them in with your branding. If you are an author, you might blog about the new novel you are developing, or even the new story you want to place in an anthology.

Announcement and News

Do you have any big news to tell the world? Your blog is the perfect place to do it. Let people know your latest news regarding you and your brand. The author in these examples might want to blog about any upcoming book releases or launch parties. They can blog about selling the rights to their book to a movie producer.

Anything newsworthy and announcement worthy about the brand would work well in these sort of posts. Keep in mind though that the news you post doesn't always have to be about you and your brand. Look at some of the other things in the news that affect your particular field and post about them.

If you are an author, you might want to blog about a new bookstore opening. Changes in the publishing field, new books from friends, peers, or authors you admire. The sky is the limit. Just look for newsworthy pieces and announcements that will fit within the realm of your brand.

Brand

This type of post is directly about your brand and what you are offering, no matter what that might be. You will base these posts around your brand. You could give an insider's look into what you do on a daily basis and who you are. It could be a view on something that you base on your values and opinions, which should already be a part of your branding. The blog simply helps to reinforce your brand and values.

Since this is a book on building a personal brand, you might imagine I'd say that all posts should be ultra brand-centric. That's not the case at all though. Having other types of posts is important to add diversity to your site and to make it interesting.

You wouldn't want to keep coming back to read a blog that just kept hitting on the same exact subjects and points, and your readers do not want that either.

Event

This is similar to announcement blogging, but this has more of a narrow focus. With this type of blog post, you let your readers know about an event that involves you, them, your brand and more. It could be an online event, a book or product launch, a signing, and more.

Here's something else to remember. Even though your site might be about you and your brand, the event doesn't necessarily have to have anything to do with you. You can always blog about other types of events, as long as they work with the type of blog and brand you have. For example, you could blog about a concert, a sporting event, a conference, and so much more!

Once you go to the event, you can actually do yet another blog post about it to let people know what happened and how things went! This gives you more content for your site and it lets people see what happened at the event. Make sure you add some photos if possible.

Guests

Do you have to be the one to write all of the blog posts on your site? While you might want to write the majority of the posts, it can actually be a good idea to have a guest blogger working with you sometimes.

The guest can write a post that falls into any one of these other categories. It provides you with extra content on your site, and some of the fans of the guest blogger will undoubtedly find your site based on that post. This can help to get more eyes on your blog and your brand.

It's also good for the guest blogger, as he or she will be able to show some great content to your audience, and that might help him or her to garner a few more fans and followers.

You can usually find guest bloggers quite easily, but you do need to be careful about whom you choose. Later in the chapter, I'll go over all of the benefits of guest bloggers and how tochoose a guest blogger that's right for your site.

How To

These types of posts are very popular. They can provide your readers with quite a bit of value too. Find some things that might interest your readers and then teach them how to do it. This could be anything you like, as long as it makes sense for your brand.

An author might let readers know how to write their own mystery story, or even how to upload a file to Nook or Kindle. Someone who blogs about videogames might have a how to article that lets their readers know how to find secrets in a game or how to beat levels and boss characters in a game.

You can surely find quite a few areas in your niche that could be prime territory for some howto posts. They are an excellent choice for blogs, and they are the types of posts that your readers are readily willing to share.

Insight

I've mentioned this before multiple times in this book, and I can't say it enough. You are a unique person. Your particular point of view gives you a different way of seeing things and different views and ideas. With these sorts of blogs, you can share your insights on things that are important to you and that will reflect your brand and the values your brand holds dear.

Sharing insights is not always easy, and it often requires quite a bit of thought and research so you can speak on topics with some authority. You might not want to jump into blogging with these types of posts.

Find the topics that interest you the most and then do your research so you can write about them with actual insight that illuminates the minds of your readers.

Interview

Another great idea for blogs is interviews. You can interview others in your field, your peers, experts, and more. Find people who are in tangential fields and interview them as well. Having an interview blog on your site a few times a month is a great idea, and it ensures you have fresh content that keeps your readers coming back for more.

By choosing great people to interview that have some type of association with what you do and what you stand for, you will be able to use those interviews to help build your brand.

Once again, we'll go back to the author example. As an author, you can interview other authors, artists, publishers, and agents. No matter your field, consider some of the type of people you might be able to interview that your audience might find interesting.

Link and Resource

Sometimes, you don't need to write a long post. You might've come across a few interesting links over the course of a week or so, and you might want to share those links with your readers.

As long as those links are items that have some type of relation to your site and blog, and you really feel as though your readers would appreciate them, you can post them. However, make sure that you check the links for their quality before you send someone else there.

Don't simply repost links without actually visiting the site and knowing that it contains the type of info and content your readers will actually find helpful. In addition, check the links on your posts every few months, just to see if they are still active and unbroken. Many times, a site will no longer exist and the links lead your visitors to limbo. Make sure they are always working.

Give the readers a bit of information about the links and resources too. No one will click a link blindly. Just a sentence or two should be fine. Let them know about the site and what they will find when they arrive. This will give them more confidence when it comes to clicking on the link.

These can be a great choice for posts when you are running short on time and don't have the ability to write a full post. However, you do not want to overuse these types of posts. If you have several of these a week without other types of posts, it smacks of laziness.

List

Everyone loves lists. I do, you do, and you can be sure your readers do as well. You can create lists any time of year, and they can be about nearly anything you like. You will want to make sure they have some type of relation to your brand in most cases though.

You can take several approaches when it comes to list posts. One might start with a problem or question they need to answer and solve. The list would be the things they can do to solve that problem. The readers of the blog, who have the same question or problem, can get the answers they need from that list.

Another type of list might simply be something that you like or even your opinion. For example, you might create a list of the ten best mystery novels of 2013 or the top superhero movies of all time.

List posts are good opportunities to engage with the readers too. They will often have their own ideas that they feel should be on the list, and they will likely leave comments on the post.

Consider some of the different sorts of lists you could use:

- Top 10 (or number of your choice) lists
- 10 (or number of your choice) Best Ways to Succeed in....
- Favorite list – list the things you love about…
- Warnings list – list the dangers of …

This is only a small sample. Lists are a great way to get people to talk on your site, and that's just what you want from your blog.

Live

Live blogging is not something everyone will want to try. It's not always easy, and it takes some dedication. Live blogging is real time updating from some event or activity, and it can sometimes take your attention away from the event.

Some people will live blog from places such as the San Diego Comic Convention, or even the Oscars. If you are going to live blog, you have to commit to it, and you have to let everyone know that you will be doing it well in advance of the date. This ensures people are reading those posts.

In today's world, live blogging is popular, but you might find that using live Tweeting through Twitter is actually easier to do, and it can actually help you to get more eyes on your brand. Later, I'll go over how to get going on Twitter.

Meme

No, you don't talk about all of the popular memes on the web with this type of post. Instead, you are actually trying to start your own meme. Ask a question on your site, and then give your answer or opinion to that question. Ask other bloggers to take the same question and answer it on their own blogs, giving you credit for being the original poster.

These are easy to do, but you don't want to overdo them. You can't continually rely on other bloggers to help you with these. Still, when you have a good and provocative question you are posting, or a fun question, it has the potential to pass to many different sites on the web.

Photo

Although you might want to put photos on quite a few of your posts, these particular types of blog posts are different – they use photos almost exclusively. The photos are the bulk of the post rather than just an addition.

Most of the time, you will have captions on the photos, although that is not necessary. If you are going to add captions, you should try to add at least one keyword to those captions, as long as they make sense.

You have all the choices in the world when it comes to the type of photo or photos you use for these posts. Of course, as with everything you do on your blog, it's smart to make sure you are using photos that help to solidify your brand.

Piggybacking

You don't have to pull your topics out of the ether and match them to your brand. Look to all of the current events in the world, as well as what might be happening in pop culture, the news, and similar places. Take those popular topics and see how you might be able to spin them to deal with your brand or niche in some way.

You aren't taking content – you never simply take content – you are looking at some of the things that are popular and then piggybacking or jumping onto the bandwagon of those things.

Story

Story blogging is different from creating your personal brand's story, but the overall idea is actually very similar. With this type of blogging, you are taking actual stories that happened in your life and you are relaying them to the readers.

The stories don't necessarily have to deal with you. If you have permission, you could tell the story of someone else and tie in how it relates to your brand. You might even want to interview that person for a later blog post.

If you are a fiction writer – or even if you aren't – you can actually include some fictionalized stories in your blog in order to get certain points across.

If you aren't a storywriter and that's not the focus of your site, you will want to preface the stories so people know they are fictional. Otherwise, you could run into some issues if people think those stories are real and find out later that they are just stories.

I feel that stories are a great idea for some of your blogs. They can be very powerful and they can stir up emotions in people relatively easily.

Survey/Questionnaire

These types of posts are great. They can provide you with some great information on your readers as well as what they think and want, and it can really help to get the dialogue started on your site.

You can offer a questionnaire or survey on your site. Have the readers respond in the comments. This gives you more insight into the readers, and your readers are your target audience after all. This information can help you when you are configuring and honing your brand.

Review

Whether this is a solicited review or one that you do independently, these can be great for getting more eyes on your blog. Review some type of product or service that would interest your target audience.

It is important to make sure you are honest in your review. This can feel a bit odd for many bloggers when they first start coming across products that are just not good. You probably don't want to hurt anyone's feelings by giving something a bad review. However, honesty and transparency are vital for the success of your blog. If you give a good, or even a decent review to a product that doesn't deserve it, your readers are no longer going to trust you. They won't trust your opinion, and all of the work you've done to build their trust will be gone.

If you don't feel comfortable giving honest reviews, I would suggest not doing the review posts.

Video

People really do enjoy video posts, and research shows that when a site has video on it, more people are likely to stay on the site longer. They are more willing to watch videos than they are to read long blog posts. Does this mean you should only shoot video posts? No, but it does mean that switching things up from time to time could be a good idea for you.

When it comes to the content of the posts, you can cover nearly anything you like, and you can do video versions of the same types of written posts you would normally do. You can be as creative as you want to be.

You do not need to have a professional camera to create these videos, but you do want to make sure the videos are clear and that the audio is good. In fact, audio is the most important aspect of the videos. If the audio is terrible, no one will want to see your video.

Tips for Blog Post Ideas

You need to have some great ideas for your posts, and they are easier to develop than you might think. Once I show you how to come up with some great ideas for your posts, I will pass along some great tips to help make the actual writing of the posts a bit easier for you.

Coming Up with Ideas

The different types of blog posts I've covered earlier in the chapter will give you plenty of different styles of posts that you can use. However, you still need to come up with the actual topics for the post. In the beginning, this is something that causes quite a bit of consternation in bloggers. They have some great ideas for the first month or so, but then feel as though they've tapped all of the subjects for their niche.

Nonsense!

It's not difficult to come up with tons of great ideas. I find that it's helpful to spend some time each week coming up with a list of topics. This helps ensure the well never runs dry and you always have something to write about for your blog. Here's a list of some ways that I've used, and that I know will be successful for you as well.

- Keep a notebook with you, or jot ideas down in your phone. If you are like me, you often have ideas at the most random times. Have a way to record those ideas.

- Have a brainstorming session and consider the things you would have liked to know more about in your niche. Consider some people you might be able to interview. Come up with some list ideas. Take one idea and branch off from that to see just how many posts you might be able to get out of it.

- I'll be back! Do a sequel to one of your most popular posts. It's already proven popular on your site, and if you have more information that you can impart, it makes sense to do another post.

- Think outside of the box. Look for different types of connections you can make between your brand and something that might seem disparate from it at first.

- Think about ways you want to help your audience and develop posts that focus on those areas.

- Ask your readers for feedback on the types of posts they would like to see in the future.

- Always look at the news in your field to keep abreast of everything that's happening. News is a great source of new content that keeps on giving and giving.

✅ Use tools such as Google News, Twitter Search and Trends, and Google Analytics to give you insight into what people might want.

Writing Useful Content

If you are writing just to write and to fill up space on your blog, it will show in the writing. You need to make sure that the post is somehow making your readers' day better. It has to inform them or inspire them. It needs to entertain or give them something that they can't find elsewhere.

Show Don't Tell

In the section on telling your story, I mentioned the importance of showing and not telling in your writing. This is true of your blog posts too. By using powerful words that evoke a visual style. Write with passion. If you've chosen your brand and your niche well, writing with passion should be easy, since you should be covering a topic you are actually passionate about in your posts.

Easy to Understand

The posts you write don't have to have the complexity of a doctoral thesis. In fact, I'm telling you right now that they shouldn't. You want the posts you write to be as simple as possible for your readers to understand. You don't want to write down to anyone, but you don't need to use large words when simpler words can get the point across just as effectively.

Make It Easy on the Eyes

No one likes the thought of reading the dreaded "wall of text" that so many sites today still have. If you want to have readers actually read your posts, you want to make them easy to skim. Keep the paragraphs short, add some lists, use plenty of headlines and break it up so it does not look daunting to read.

Make the Post Visual

Instead of simply adding text, try to add a photo to your posts. While you don't need to add a photo to all of the posts you write, they really do help to add some visual appeal. Whenever you can, add a photo as long as it makes sense for the post you are writing.

A Call to Action

At the end of the blog post, you want to request that the readers do something. It could be something as simple as commenting and adding their thoughts about the post to your comments section. You might ask them to sign up to your newsletter or subscribe to your blog. Maybe you want them to follow you on Twitter or Facebook. The call to action can be anything, and it can be different from post to post.

Do all posts absolutely need to have a call to action? They don't, but you will find that the posts that have one generally get more results for you. Readers, if they like what they've seen, will often comply with the call to action as long as it is something simple for them to do.

Proof Before Posting

Just as you do with any of the content you have – for your site, blog, social networks, print, and more – you need to be sure it is in good shape. This means you have to reread it before you post it, and you need to make sure your grammar and spelling are up to par.

Sure, mistakes always slip through in writing. However, with some simple proofing, you can eliminate quite a few of them. Here are a few ways to do it, and I highly suggest you do these with every single post you write.

- Reread the post
- Read the post aloud, or have a computer program read the post to you

✅ Have someone else read the post
✅ Scan the post for errors right before you hit publish
✅ Read the post once more when it is live

Even with all of that attention, there is a chance something can slip by you. When that happens, don't worry. Chances are good you will have an eagle-eyed reader who is more than willing to let you know where you made your mistake. Thank the reader for pointing it out and then fix the error.

What Schedule Works for You?

How often should you post? You don't have to post every day, or even several days a week, but I feel you really should at least try to post once a week. Any less than that, and it could cause you to lose readers. People have limited attention spans and countless things to keep them happy and busy online. The more quality content you can provide the better.

Once you have your schedule, you have to make sure you can stick to it. Readers will come to your blog expecting a new post on certain days, and they won't be happy if it isn't there.

Keep Writing

You might not see the traction from your blog that you want right in the beginning. It can take time to build an audience. Keep writing and keep creating good content, and make sure that you are posting regularly. This will help to ensure you are getting better placement in the search engines, and more people will start to find you thanks to all of your other branding efforts.

As you write, you will notice that something else is happening too. You are actually getting better at writing. Even if you aren't a great writer currently, you will get better if you keep practicing. You will develop your own style that is distinctive to you and thus to your brand.

Keep writing and the readers will come to you.

What Makes a Guest Blogger a Good Idea?

Guest blogging has become extremely popular over the past few years, and it actually does have a wealth of benefits. Guest bloggers can help to ease the burden on you needing to come up with all of the content on your site. They can come up with some great content that helps to get more people reading your blog. It provides some different perspectives and insights from others in your field.

Although you will still be the one who writes most of the content for your site, a guest blogger can be very valuable for you.

Tips for Choosing a Guest Blogger

You never simply want to hand your blog off to someone you don't know. You have to know the abilities of the writer before you let them write for your site, and you certainly need to know what topic they will be using in their post. You always need to know and agree to the topics and the themes well in advance.

When you have your topics agreed upon well in advance of when the post will appear, it gives the blogger time to write on the topic and to put in the proper research. It also ensures you won't have any duplicate topics on your site in the same week!

Be Choosy

You don't have to choose just any blogger for your site. You have the time to be selective about the guest blogger you choose. In fact, it is very important that you take the time to seek out the perfect blogger who complements your brand, even though you might have differing opinions on certain things.

Once you start to develop your brand and your blog starts to get more popular, you will not have to search for guest bloggers. They will start to seek you out. The trouble with this is that some of the requests you get from bloggers who want to write for your blog is the quality they bring to the table. Often, they will not have as much cachet as you have in the field. You need to verify the quality of the content they offer before you post it to your site.

Let Them Know What You Need

Guest bloggers aren't mind readers. You have to let them know what you expect when you have them write a post for you. For example, if you want to have images in all of your posts, let the writer know. If you have the time, you can provide the image that's appropriate to the post, or you could have the blogger do it.

If you don't want any self-promotion in the post, then you need to let the blogger know. You should still let them have a place to include a very short bio and a link to their own site. You could even come up with a standard bio style for your guest bloggers to use, so all of them follow the same style.

If you plan to use guest bloggers regularly, it's a good idea to come up with a style guide for the bloggers. This ensures that they are all on the same page when creating posts and covering various topics and you will not have to worry as much about posts that don't match what you need.

Once they write their articles, make sure you give them constructive feedback on the pieces, especially if you plan to use them again. Focus on the positive, but make sure they know about any areas where they might need work on future posts.

Could You Guest Blog?

One of the reasons so many people like the idea of guest blogging is so they can spread their own brand influence. You can use guest blogging in the same way. Start looking for other blogs similar to your own, or that are in the same or similar niche and offer your services as a guest poster.

You need to adhere to the same types of rules that you would expect a guest blogger to your site to follow. Write great content, follow the site's guidelines, and make sure the blog owner is happy with what you provide.

Once you start to develop more of a following on your own blog, you will find that getting gigs as a guest blogger is generally much easier. Some blog owners might even come to you and ask if you would like to write a post on their blog.

Make the Most of Your Content

Those who blog regularly have to come up with a substantial amount of great content all the time. The content can do more than just sit on your site and help you get hits though. You can reuse the information in a number of different ways. Some of the things you could use the content for include:

- Creating an e-book or a printed book
- Using it for an audio podcast
- Creating videos based on the content
- Using abbreviated versions of the content in a newsletter

Everyone Has a Strategy

Different bloggers have different strategies for success. The one truth about blogging is that the same thing will probably not work for all people. There is no "perfect" formula. However, the above tips are some of the basics that most bloggers today utilize. Use those and then cultivate your own strategy that works with your brand.

Blogging is not too hard, and it can actually be extremely fun. You can use the blog to better your SEO rank, reach out to people, and to get your brand out there and into the world.

Of course, you have to have a blog set up to make all of this happen. It's time to get up close and personal with WordPress.

Setting Up a WordPress Blog and Getting Started

In this section, I'll teach you everything you need to know about getting your blog up and running on WordPress. It is very easy to do, and I imagine you'll even have some fun setting up your blog and starting to connect your brand to the world.

Why WordPress?

With so many blogging platforms out there, you might be wondering why I'm focusing on WordPress. I've found that Word-Press is extremely simple to set up and use, it has a number of features and options so you can set up the blog the way you need.

It also happens to be one of the most popular platforms when it comes to blogging. You can find plenty of other tutorials and forums online from people using WordPress, just in case you have any questions I don't answer here.

WordPress might not be the only option out there, but is the one that I recommend highly.

- Easy, robust content management system
- Cost effective
- Highly customizable
- Easy to use with a small learning curve

Now that you see more of the benefits it offers, it's time that I lead you deeper into WordPress!

GetGoing with WordPress

I'll provide you with the information you need to get started, but I also feel you should do even more learning on your own. The more you know about the platform and the system the better.

A great place to go is codex.wordpress.org. It features tons of great information I believe you will find useful. I'll cover all of the basics here, but the information on that site can help you learn even more about WP, including some simple troubleshooting methods.

Instead of using the free-hosted WordPress service, most serious bloggers will want to have a self-hosted blog, simply because they have so much more control over it. Many new to blogging feel that self-hosting is going to be difficult, but that's not the case at all.

Your Domain

First, make sure you know what domain name you want to use and make sure it is open. You can actually register your domain when you set up your account and host, but if you've already registered your domain name, there's no need to worry.

Your Host

You need to choose your host. At the end of this section, I'll go over the pros and cons of cloud hosting and dedicated server hosting. Countless hosting options are available. You could choose companies such as Yahoo, GoDaddy, Bluehost, and others. Most of the hosts are relatively cheap and all of them are easy to use. However, you should make sure the host will work well with WordPress. Research the host you are considering and check out all of their options.

When you are choosing your host, they will generally give you the option of registering your domain through them. In those cases, you simply type in the domain you want, and the host does the rest of the work. It is very fast and very easy.

If you've already registered your domain, you can still use it with your new host. However, the hosts may have slightly different processes when it comes to connecting with your domain. Make sure you follow the instructions from your particular host when you are trying to get your domain up and running with your site. Most of the time, it's just a few simple steps. It can take between 24 and 48 hours for those changes to take effect though.

Installing WordPress

The host you choose will likely have a one-click install button for installing WordPress, which makes getting started with the platform that much easier. While it is possible to install it from scratch, it's not something I would recommend for those who have never blogged before and who know very little about computers. The one-click install is fast, simple, and the way I recommend.

Once you install the platform, you will be able to access it through your host. You can change the look of the blog, write posts, approve comments, and much more. The learning curve to get up and running is quite low.

However, WordPress is a robust system that offers a bounty of tools and features that can help to make your blog truly unique. To go over all of them would take an entire book in and of itself. I will touch on some of the most important aspects of the platform though. The more you use the system the more features you will want to start using for your blog.

Choosing a Theme

What do you want your blog to look like? Take some time to cruise around the web and look at a number of different types of blogs. Look at the features you like and don't like. Look at the color schemes and see how they work with the branding on those sites. All of the sites look different, even though they are all running the WordPress platform.

They can do this because they utilize themes. The themes are the background and the architecture that provides the look and the feel of the sites. Even though a dozen sites might be using the same theme, they can tweak and change those themes, add their own graphics, change the colors, alter the layout, and much more to help make it unique to them.

That's the beauty and power of themes, and that is why so many people are flocking to WordPress. It is also one of the reasons that I am recommending it to you.

However, with all of the choices and options when it comes to themes, that does mean that you could run the risk of choosing the wrong theme for your site. I'm here to make sure that doesn't happen.

Writing Articles

In addition to creating posts for your blog, you might also want to see if you can write some posts or articles for other sites. Find sites and other brands similar to your own and see if they might be open to exchanging posts and articles. Make sure you ask if you can link back to your own site from the article.

This increases the number of links you have back to your site, and as you should know by now, having more links can help to ensure a better page ranking.

The articles you create need to do several things in order to be effective. The articles must:

- Be informative
- Be well written
- Be in line with your brand

This helps to get more attention for your site and for your brand. Writing articles also helps with furthering the goal of becoming an expert in the eyes of the readers. Having that expert status – regardless of what you are trying to do with your brand – can really help you further your career.

Free, Premium, or Custom

First, you have to decide whether you want to use one of the free themes, a premium theme, or a custom theme. Let's look at the difference.

- ✅ **Free** – As the name suggests, these themes are free. While free might sound like the perfect price, these themes are limited in what they can do in most cases. You have less control over how they look, and you might not be able to create one that's right for your branding purposes. Free is generally not a good idea if you are a serious blogger.

- ✅ **Premium** – This will be a great choice for serious bloggers. You have a wealth of different options, and the premium themes are generally very affordable. You can have a theme that has tons of great options and features. The premium themes can give you much more control over how your blog looks. Of course, it will take a bit of work on your part to understand all of the options those themes are actually able to offer.

- ✅ **Custom** – These will provide you the most flexibility, but they do not come cheaply. You will need to hire and actual designer and let him or her know what you need for your site. They can create a theme from scratch, or they can customize a theme already in existence for you. If you have the money and the time, this is a viable option. However, with the amount of choices you have with the premium themes, it really isn't necessary. I would suggest that you tried it on your own for the first blog you create.

Do Your Research

Thousands of themes are available today, and that means you have some research cut out for you. Most of the sites that offer themes will have a good search feature so you can change the search parameters to find a theme that most closely matches the vision of your site.

In the beginning, I would suggest simply looking at all of the different available themes and only narrow your search after you have a better idea of the options available.

As you start to look at the themes, compile a list of the features that you really want to have, and the features that you need. Then, you will be able to use the search parameters to locate the themes that most closely represent your ideal.

Make sure the theme has all of the pages and features you need and that it has the functionality your site will require. For example, while not all personal branding sites will need to have a shopping cart, yours might. Make sure your theme is able to handle that before you buy it and find out that it doesn't!

Always make sure you read the reviews on any theme you are considering. Look to see what other users have to say about the functionality of the theme and how easy it is to use. If the theme is particularly new, and you can't find any reviews for it yet, I suggest waiting on that theme. If you really like it, you can bookmark it and visit it again in a few months to see some reviews from other users.

Some of the most popular places to look for blog themes today include:

- WooThemes
- ThemeForest
- Elegant Themes
- Template Monster

They are not the only companies that have themes available, however, they are a safe company to browse. Many of the theme sites on the web today are hiding malware, viruses, and other terrible things you don't want to encounter. Stick with the reputable sites and you should be safe.

What Does the Theme Offer?

When you are searching for a theme, look at all of the features it offers and compare that with what you want for your site. We'll look at some of the most important features that you will most assuredly want with your theme.

- **Responsive Design** – This simply means your site will display on various types of devices and still look great. Since you never know what people will be using to view your site, it makes sense that you would want a design that will look great in mobile phones, tablets, laptops, and desktops. With all of the people using mobile devices to access the web today, this is a highly important feature that I feel every blog should have.

- **Social** – Just as being mobile friendly is important, it is important to be social friendly as well. You need to make sure that your theme is able to feature icons from all of the social media sites you use. You want the social icons to be prominent and easy to see, since you want visitors to your site to start following you on social media as well. After all, it's all about branding and social media is a vital aspect of that today.

- **Simple to Navigate** – The site needs to be simple for your visitors to use and navigate. You don't want a complex, labyrinthine site that is difficult use. By keeping things "lightweight" with the theme, you can also ensure the pages load faster. In today's world of faster is better, this is important if you want to keep the attention of your audience.

Does It Come with Documentation?

When you are getting a WordPress theme, you need to make sure it comes with documentation. Documentation will let you know everything the theme has to offer, so you know all of the features it has and how to use all of those features.

You do not want to spend an inordinate amount of time trying to figure out how to get to all of the functions your theme offers. Good documentation will be nice and clear and make it easy to understand how to use the theme. Whether you want to know how to change the background color of the theme, or you want to know how to add another column, all of the info should be in the documentation.

What about Support?

Is there any type of support with the theme? Many developers, even independent developers, will add support for their theme, but some don't have the time or the resources to do that. This means you could run into issues getting help if you have trouble with the theme.

Often, there are communities of people using the same theme though, and they can provide guidance and support if you need it. Always make sure you understand exactly what is available when it comes to support.

In the case of custom themes, you really don't have to worry about this because you will have direct access to the developer who can help you get things running and make sure you understand how to use the theme.

Creating Headers and Footers for WordPress Themes

Creating a custom header and footer for your blog is a great idea, and it can really help you with your branding efforts. Changing the appearance of the header doesn't necessarily require that you have a specialist help you either.

Many of the themes you find for WordPress allow users to up-load custom headers and footers easily. It's simply uploading a file. This allows you to have a personalized look to your site.

When you are looking for themes you are considering pur-chasing, make sure that you look to see if they offer the option for custom image headers.

Once you have your theme installed, go into the Appearance section of your blog and then click on Header. This will let you browse your computer for the file you want to upload. You could also choose an image from the Media Library on your blog.

Different themes may require that the header is a certain size, such as 1000 pixels wide. Always check the requirements for your theme so you can then create a custom header that will fit properly. Using an image that is exactly the right size will always give you the best results.

Keep in mind that you can only upload certain file types:

- ✔ .jpeg
- ✔ .gif
- ✔ .png

When it comes to creating the look of your header, you can use Photoshop and other editing programs as long as they can produce files in one of the three formats mentioned above. If you need to have any transparency in the image, you need to use a .png or a .gif.

What happens if the image you want to use for the header isn't the right size? Don't worry about it! The tools in WordPress will allow you to crop the image and use the part that you need. This is not ideal – I feel you should do your best to create a true custom header that reflects your brand – it is a viable so-lution for those who want to get a blog up and running quickly.

When it comes to what you should put on your header or footer, it really depends on your brand as well as what it is that you are trying to do.

Some good options might be your personal logo, if you have one, images of places, items, and products that represent you and your brand, or even a photo of you. You have endless options. Just make sure that you choose something that actually reflects your personal brand.

Code for the Header and Footer

With your headers and footers, you can also add HTML code very easily. Just click on the header and footer areas in your blog settings and apply the code for Google, analytics, ads, or anything else you might want to add to the site. Make sure you test the responsiveness of the code you add though. It should work by simply copying and pasting, but always double-check to make sure it is working properly.

You can put many things in your footers, including:

- Copyright notice
- Contact information
- Links
- Logos

How to Create and Add a Favicon to Your Site

You've probably seen favicons around and wondered just how you could get one for your own site. Fortunately, it's actually quite simple to do when you are using WordPress.

Favicon is a term that is slang for "favorites icon". You normally see these icons in the favorite's section once you favorite or bookmark a site. Not all sites have them, but they can be quite useful as a quick visual way to identify a site. It's another way to brand your site visually, and that's always a good thing!

The favicon generally measures 16 x 16 pixels, and you will save it in the favicon.ico root directory of your server. If you have access to the root directories, you can save them with any WordPress blog.

Creating the Favicon

The image you create can be anything that you like, but since this book is about personal branding, it's probably a good idea to choose something such as a logo, or some other image that people will come to associate with your brand. You can use Photoshop, GIMP, and other image editing software that lets you save .ico files.

Make sure you are working with a square image that is 16 x 16 pixels and place the logo or other image into that space, or resize it. Save your file as favicon.ico and place it into the correct root directory. The reason you want to use .ico if you can, rather than a .png or .gif is because all of the browsers will support the format, so all browsers can see your favicon.

If you don't have one of those programs, you do have another option for creating the favicon. You can use faviconer.com, which lets you create your favicon right on their site. It's a great solution for those who don't have the other program. You can import images easily, and it already has the perfect sized space – 16 x 16 for regular favicon.ico files and 32 x 32 for retina display.

If you want to add your favicon quickly and easily without getting into the root folders, you have an option for that too. I recommend the plugin "All in One Favicon", which you can download from WordPress for your blog.

This plugin will add the favicon to your site and it will support the .ico files, as well as .png and .gif. It's one of the fastest and easiest ways to get the icon on your site with no fuss.

Should you Choose a Cloud or Dedicated Server

Quite a few people are arguing about the benefits of cloud hosting versus the benefits of using a dedicated server. Both the cloud and dedicated servers can have their benefits and drawbacks.

Instead of telling you which one you need to use, since there are so many variables from one person to another, I will give you a rundown of the features of each and give you suggestions on when you might want to use one rather than the other.

What is Cloud Hosting?

It seems as though everyone in the world is talking about the cloud and cloud hosting. Amazon is using it, and so is Apple. The new videogame systems are looking into ways to use cloud computing as well. Many websites and blogs today also utilize the power of the cloud.

What does that really mean though? It means that the servers are in a virtual environment. The cloud utilizes a large number of different servers to accomplish this. The people who are on the cloud servers are renting virtual space instead of space on regular physical servers.

Generally, there are shared and dedicated servers for hosting, and cloud hosting is something of a bridge between the two that offers the best of both worlds. The cost is less than dedicated hosting, but you have more control and safety than you would with a regular shared host.

With cloud hosting, you can upscale and downscale easily as you need, which makes it a truly flexible system. This ties in directly with the cost effectiveness of the system. People are enjoying the cloud hosting options because they are relatively easy to set up and they are very reliable.

Since there are so many servers running the cloud systems, an issue in one doesn't mean a catastrophe. It simply means the resources will shift to another server, and your visitors should not notice any hiccups in their experience.

This type of host is generally good for most bloggers out there today. If you have an extremely popular site and you have a large number of visitors each day, it might be time to think about moving to a dedicated server.

What is a Dedicated Server?

These are the traditional sorts of servers, and they can work well for large websites and very popular blogs that have a substantial amount of traffic. However, it's worth noting that the cost of the dedicated server is generally quite a bit higher than cloud hosting will be. If you don't need the space and power of a dedicated server quite yet, I suggest that you stick with cloud hosting. The server could cost between $100 and $500 a month, and in some cases, quite a bit more. Upwards of $1,000 for some large sites is actually common.

If you feel you need one of the dedicated servers, make sure you shop around to find the best deals possible on the service.

In addition to the added cost, you will need to have someone actually set up the dedicated server. The company you hire can do this. However, with cloud servers, you can handle everything on your own very easily.

The Performance and Reliability

Both cloud hosting and dedicated servers can provide you with high quality performance. Both are fast. However, with the cloud servers, you will generally find more reliability. That's because you don't have to worry about the machine going down since the information is on multiple virtual servers.

If the dedicated server were to crash, you may not have a back-up in place, and that means your visitors will not actually be able to access your site.

When you look at the information I've provided on these two options, it's easy to see which one is likely to be in your best interest – cloud hosting. It's cheaper, it's more reliable, and it's perfect for those who are just starting out with their blog, just as you are doing.

Creating Your Site with the Right Stuff

Your website or blog site needs to be the central launch point for your brand in today's world. Most people have access to the web, and they will likely connect with you through your site. Some might find you through social media, which I will go over in the next section.

However, having a virtual base of operations that can communicate your brand, and connect visitors with your other online locations, is essential.

You can create a website on your own if you want, or you may want to hire a professional to do the work. It all depends on your budget and the level of skill you possess, not to mention the amount of time you have. Setting up a blog is quick and easy, and you do not need to have any special skills to get up and running with a blog quickly.

The site needs to include a number of things in order to be effective, and all of those things need to further your brand. The site needs:

- Your branded story/bio
- Information on what you offer – links to your books, DVDs, etc.
- Your skills, education, and anything that makes you special or unique

✅ At least one photo of you

✅ Links to articles or guest blog posts you've written, as well as to sites with information about you

✅ Links to all of your social media sites including Twitter, Facebook, LinkedIn, Pinterest, YouTube, etc.

✅ In some cases, you may want to place your branded CV on the site as well.

Making the Most of the Social Networks

Social media is inescapable today. Most people have a presence on at least one or two of the most popular social media sites. Anyone who wants to build a personal brand knows the importance of having a strong presence on the social networks. Some of the networks you need to become a part of include:

 Twitter

 Facebook

 LinkedIn

Some of the sites that might be right for you:

 Google Plus

 Pinterest

 Instagram

In addition, look for any specialty sites that might work with your particular career or the way you are trying to brand yourself. For example, Stage 32 is a relatively new social network that connects people who are in the entertainment field, such as screenwriters, directors, producers, etc.

The Best Practices for Social Networking

Many who are new to social media do not really understand how it works. It is not merely a tool for advertising yourself incessantly. Later in the book, I will go over some of the worst things you can do that can kill your social media.

The following are some of the "best practices" for social media interactions. Adhere to these guidelines. You should have no trouble mastering social media and propelling your brand when you do.

- ✅ **Follow and Interact** – when someone connects with you, or you connect with someone, on one of the social media sites, you should make sure to interact with them. Connecting with the audience is important when growing your brand.

- ✅ **Be Social** – you don't want to keep advertising what you have to offer. You want to be social, not a constant commercial. Try to connect with your audience.

- ✅ **Keep Your Tone Geared to Your Brand** – make sure your posts and interactions are in line with your brand, and that they don't go too far off topic. For example, you have your own political opinions. People who might follow you or even hire you have their opinions. You have to be careful about what you share, especially if it has nothing to do with your brand.

- ✅ **Have Something to Add** – if you have something constructive to add to a conversation, jump in and talk. If you don't have anything to say, you should stay out of the conversation.

These tips should help you to get a good handle on most of the different social networking sites people are using today. I'll give you some more tips later in the chapter.

Setting Up Accounts for the Major Social Networks

I've mentioned some of the most popular social networks, and I'm sure you are at least somewhat familiar with most of them. In this section though. I'm going to go through the top options and show you how you can set up your accounts.

Follow the simple instructions and you will have your accounts up and running for LinkedIn, Google Plus, Twitter, and Facebook in just minutes. Of course, once you are up and running on those sites, it's up to you to be active on them and to make the most of them.

Setting up a LinkedIn Account

This powerful social networking site has the professional in mind. It's possible to connect with other professionals you already know, and to widen your network and start connecting with others in your niche and other niches as well.

Getting started with an account is actually very easy.

- Head to LinkedIn.com.
- In the upper right corner of the screen, you will see the text: Join Today. Click on it.
- Type in your first name, last name, email, and the password you want to use. If you already have a Facebook account, you can actually use that account to sign up, making it even faster and easier.
- They will send you an email to confirm your account. Once you confirm the account, you can get started.
- Edit your profile by adding a photo of yourself, choosing your industry, and filling out your experience, companies you've worked for, education, qualifications, and more.

☑ You have the option to write a summary. This is something I highly suggest doing. You can use the same bio you used for your blog in this space.

☑ Add any special abilities you might have. Once you do this, others on the site can endorse you for those skills and abilities, which will help to give you more credibility.

☑ Start adding connections with people you know and people you want to know. You can search a person's name, company, and even job title to see if they are on LinkedIn.

☑ Add your blog's address, Twitter account, and more to your profile so that more people can connect with you on those other sites as well.

Setting up a Google+ Account

Google+ has quite a bit of potential, and it is different from the other social networks out there. Once you set up an account with the tips in this section, I recommend that you spend some time exploring all of the different tools and features on the site. They have a host of useful features. It's very easy to use once you get started, and you will continue to find new and fun features.

☑ Head to plus.google.com.

☑ Click on the text that reads, "Create an Account" in the top right portion of the screen.

☑ Fill in your name and other pertinent info.

☑ Choose a good profile photo. It's a good idea to use the same photo for your bio, blog, and your other social networking sites so you have a uniform look all across the web. Once you choose your photo, your account is active.

☑ Now, you have to set up your profile. Add your tagline, story, accomplishments, education, work experience, and more to your profile. It is important that you do not skip any of these areas, as all of them play a part in your branding efforts.

✅ Next, you will build Circles, and this is where Google+ is different from other sites. A Circle is simply a way to categorize the different people in your life. You could have a Circle for family, a Circle for Coworkers, a Circle for fans, and more. You can have as many as you like, but I'd suggest keeping the number down so you can manage them more easily. You can also determine which Circles see different content that you post.

✅ Like the other social networking sites, you can post content. You do not have a word limit as you do on Twitter. Add video, links, photos, and more to the content you share.

Setting up a Facebook Account

Facebook is still the biggest of the social networks. Most people, including the majority of those who are in your target audience, are probably on the site. It's a great way to connect, and you will find that Google gives FB and other sites quite a bit of credence when it comes to search results. Thus, having an account can actually make it easier for people to find and connect with you.

✅ Go to facebook.com

✅ You will see a signup box. Type in your information – name, email, password, sex, and birth date. Click the sign-up button.

✅ You can then confirm your account through the email address.

Fill in your information – add your education, work experience, military experience, location, etc.

✅ You can then start sending friend requests to people that you know.

✅ Upload a profile picture – the same one that you are using for your other social media sites and your blog.

✔ Edit your profile in the "Edit My Profile" section. This gives you more control over what people see and know about you including hometown, relationship status, what you are looking for, political views, favorite movies, books, television shows, and more.

✔ Fill out your profile fully and then start posting!

Setting up a Twitter Account

Twitter is one of the most popular social networks out there today, and you don't want to skip using it. When it comes to branding and connecting with others, it's a fun and simple way to make social media work for you. It might take you some time to get accustomed to the features and the "Twitter etiquette", but it is well worth the time you put into it.

✔ Visit twitter.com.

✔ Click on the text that reads, "Join the Conversation".

✔ Create your username along with your password, and then enter your email address. Try to use your real name or something close, for your username since you are using the site for branding purposes. Fill out the captcha on the page to let them know you are not a bot and hit accept to create your account. That's all there is to setting up your basic account.

✔ Start looking for people to connect with on the site. Use Twitter search to start looking for people. Twitter will eventually start recommending people you should follow, and it pays to look closely at those suggestions.

If feel so strongly that Twitter is a great option for branding and networking that I've included ten tips on making Twitter work even better for your branding that appears in the very next section. Use those tips and tools and take your Twittering to the next level!

Ten Tips for Mastering Branding on Twitter

I find Twitter to be very useful, and I happen to think Twitter is very fun. I think you will feel the same way once you get a hang of how things work on the site. Here are some great tips and tricks to help you get the most from your experience on Twitter.

- ✔ **Photo** – Use the same photo here that you are using in your blog and other social networking sites. Having an actual photo on your Twitter account gives your account more authenticity.

- ✔ **Bio** – You have room to add a very short bio. Again, distill your brand and bio down to just a few words.

- ✔ **Location** – Always add your location, as many people search by location when they are looking for people to follow.

- ✔ **URLs** – You want to connect your brand across your blog and all of your sites. The best way to do that is by adding your URLs for your websites and other social media accounts.

- ✔ **Image** – You can change the background image for your profile page, and it is important that you do. Changing out the images on your profile and using images instead is one of the best ways to bring your brand to your Twitter space. Those who look up your page will be treated to those images, so make sure you choose ones that are indicative of your brand. Use the same or similar images to those you have on your blog to create some consistency.

- ✔ **Follow** – When people follow you, make sure you follow them back. It's common courtesy.

- ✔ **Tweet** – You need to keep Tweeting, and you need to make sure those regular tweets are fun, interesting, and informative. You don't want to post inflammatory Tweets! Try to post at least three to five times a day, and post at different times of the day. Share Tweets, photos, videos, and more.

✅ **Share Information** – Share information that you have on your blog and other sites, share important news, and make sure you share the content of the other people you are following as well.

✅ **Be Careful** – You don't want to do too much promotion. Over promotion on your sites can actually cause people to stop wanting to follow you. It's bad form, so don't do it!

✅ Engage – It is important to take the time to participate in conversations and to engage on the social media site. Connect with like-minded people and those who have an interest in your brand.

How to Measure Your Social Media Success

Being on all of the social media sites is simply not enough. You also need to make sure you are getting actual results from your time on those networks. The goal is to draw more of your target audience to your social sites, and then to get them to want to learn more about you. You have to measure your success with social media, and if you are not doing as well as you hope, you have to make adjustments.

Trying to determine your ROI for your social media can be difficult, but it is possible. Here are a few good things you can do.

✅ **Listen to What People Say** – go onto the social media sites and see what people are saying about you. In Twitter, for example, you can type in your Twitter name and see conversations regarding you.

✅ **Use Analytics** – analytics tools for social media sites can give you a good indication of how you are doing. Google Analytics is a great choice and is the most powerful option for measuring your ROI with social media.

✅ **Consider the Engagement** – check to see how often your followers actually engage with the content you post. If you have very little engagement, you need to retool your content as well as what you are offering. Social networking with a great ROI generally has a lot of engagement from the followers.

Reach People Who Can Hire You with LinkedIn

One of the most powerful and helpful of the social networking sites, especially for professionals who are trying to connect with peers and other companies, is LinkedIn. Connecting with peers can be great, but you have to remember that they are on the ones who are doing the hiring.

You need to connect with hiring managers and recruiters. Many of these people will be on LinkedIn, but you will not necessarily know who they are. Thus, you need to start with some research. Use the web to search for hiring managers, HR professionals, etc., at the companies that interest you. Get the names of those individuals, and then get onto your LinkedIn account and add them to your network.

Learn what you can about the individuals so you have some information about them when you are applying for the job. By connecting with people who work at the business, you can learn quite a bit more about the company too. Remember that with this site, the quality of your connections is far more important than the quantity of connections. You need to connect with the people who can actually hire you.

Whenever you are contacting someone through the site, make sure you are professional and respectful. You are making connections, but you do not want to start hounding these people for work. Build those connections and relationships and let the branding work its magic.

Do You Need a Personal Logo?

If you aren't building a large corporation, do you need a logo? Many people who are just beginning their branding journey might not feel as though they need to have a logo of their own, but they can actually be very helpful. Just as with logos for companies, your personal logo can come to represent you and your brand. When your audience sees the logo, they immediately think of you and your brand.

Having your own logo can offer some great benefits, including:

- Giving you the appearance of being fully established
- Helping attract more clients, a greater audience, and even some potential employers
- Helping to solidify your brand
- Boosting your credibility and reputation

A personal logo can do all of these things and more. Do you need one? While many people can get by without a logo, if you are trying to reach the maximum potential of your brand, you really should consider creating one.

If you are planning to create a logo though, remember that it needs to reflect the brand you are building. Consider the places you will use the logo, such as your website, letterhead, social sites, and more. Make sure it will work in all of those areas and make sure it is easy enough to reproduce in print and still look great.

Help for the Logo

Great graphic design is not easy. In fact, trying to design your own personal logo might just be impossible for most people. You do not want a cookie cutter logo – you need something that suits you and your brand. The best way to get that is with a professional graphic designer. The cost for a quality logo is well worth it.

Creating a Resume with Your Brand in Mind

If you are developing your brand in an effort to get a better job, you will need to restructure your resume. You want your new resume to reflect the brand you've been building. In the beginning of the resume, you can use your personal branding statement, or a slightly longer summary, to illustrate your position and your values. One of your strongest branding tools, the statement, will be the first thing that a potential employer sees. This can help to make a good impression.

When you create a branded resume, you want to highlight those same things you highlight with your branding. The accomplishments and the skills you list should match your brand, and they should illustrate just how beneficial you will be for the job.

Try to be as enthusiastic as possible with your resume, and make sure you are using the best and most powerful descriptive words possible throughout.

One of the best techniques to use when writing a resume is to write about the things that you can offer the company and the person you are now – based on your brand, naturally. Don't try to write your resume with an eye to the future about the things you want to accomplish.

Show the employer the great things you've done and that you can do for them right now. If you have fully explored and developed your brand, it should be easy to do.

Getting Jobs through Online Followers and Friends

Thanks to social media, you can create a number of excellent connections online that have the potential to result in a new job. As long as you put in the work to find the right target audience, you can connect with people who are in the right field and at the right companies.

The followers and friends you are cultivating are a part of the audience you are targeting with your brand, and that means they might have connections in your industry. They could be great contacts to have when you are trying to get a new job.

However, that does not mean you should pester your connections about job openings at their companies. You really need to make sure you are developing real connections with the people before you question them about any job possibilities.

Let your brand shine, and make sure you are courteous and professional.

Show your followers and friends what you have to offer through your branding without constantly hitting them up for information on openings in the company. They will remember you well when you do. If you are pestering them, they will remember that too, and they will not give you the help you want in finding new employment!

If someone does help you to get a job, remember to thank the person and keep him or her in mind in case he or she needs reciprocation at some point down the line. The connections you are making should be for life, not just for the next job.

Great Places to Connect and Network Offline

Thus far, we've focused mostly on the online things you need to do for your brand, but the world is a big place and it offers more than just online interactions. You can find a number of great ways to meet and network with people in the real world too. In fact, it is important to meld your online and offline world if you want to take full advantage of your branding.

Some of the best places to connect with people in your field, or who may be a part of your target audience include:

- Workshops
- Conventions
- Trade Shows
- Volunteering at a nonprofit organization
- Start your own networking group

Keep watch for other ways to meet people who are a part of your target audience, and make sure to take advantage of any opportunities that come your way.

Use the Press

One of the best ways to continue to engage with people and brand yourself offline is by using the power of the press. Traditional media is not dead, and you can still get quite a bit of use from it with your branding. Consider the power of press releases, interviews in the newspaper, as well as on television.

If you have an interesting angle and an interesting message, there's a very good chance that you will be able to get newspapers and local television studios interested in doing an interview with you. This can do some fantastic things for your branding plan and your credibility.

Start a Meetup

If you want to connect with like-minded people who have an interest in what you have to offer and that you think might want to know more about you and your brand, start your own meetup group. It's possible to organize a get together at a restaurant, a sporting event, and more. It's a great way to get to meet more people. This can be a good start for your own networking group.

Writers will often do this. They will set up a writer's group and then help one another with different types of writing problems and issues, and they can even act as a great network of people to provide one another with more opportunities. It's possible for many different people in different niches to do similar things.

Become an Expert

Keep working at becoming an expert in your field and niche. People will start to see you as someone to trust in the field, and that can help you garner some speaking engagements, which is the perfect time to meet more people and to start networking your brand.

Brand It

Another great thing to do is to put your brand – your name, image, or logo – on items that you can give away or sell to others. This is a great way to create some goodwill amongst people and to put your brand in as many places as possible.

You do not have to spend a fortune to do this either. Find some cost effective items, such as mouse pads, wallets, and the like that might work for you. If you can find something that works well with your particular brand, that's even better.

Breaking the Ice and Getting to Know People at Events

One of the hardest things for people to do is to get to know people when they are at a convention, a signing, or any type of event. Some people feel shy when it comes to speaking with others. Others simply don't know the best ways to break the ice without coming across as obnoxious.

It doesn't have to be as scary and as difficult as you might think it is at first. You can use the following tips to help you stand out and to meet others when you are at any type of event.

Here are some ways you can do that.

Smile

Smiling is very important. It shows that you are open and friendly, and that it is okay for people to approach you. When you smile, you will also find that it is easier to exude more confidence.

Even if you don't feel like smiling, do it! When you are at an event, smiling is really one of the best icebreakers possible.

Who would you rather speak with, someone smiling or someone who looks grumpy?

Listen

These events are about more than just pushing your brand and your message. Others that you want to connect with and network with will want to speak to you. They will have their own stories to tell. It is important that you listen to them. Answer any questions they have, engage with them in person just as you would if you were on a social network with someone.

Simply listening to someone can really make him or her see that you have an interest in what he or she has to say. In today's busy world, listening is a skill that seems to be vanishing.

Talk

Just as you have to listen, you also need to make sure you are talking when the time is appropriate. You should make sure you are staying on message and on brand with whatever you have to say.

However, you should have more than just your branding message coming out of your mouth. If the only thing you are doing is pushing your brand at these events, you will find that it can quickly become tiresome for people.

You have fun and interesting stories. Use these to help develop an even deeper engagement with the people at these events.

Make Eye Contact

This is something that so few people today do. If you really want to connect with someone, you need to make eye contact. It is a way to communicate without speaking. It's a way to show that you are confident. When you avoid eye contact with people, some will perceive this as a weakness or shyness on your part. They may not want to have anything to do with you. Worse, they might feel as though they can take advantage of you.

If you aren't accustomed to making and holding eye contact, it can seem a bit strange at first. It can actually be difficult to hold that eye contact without breaking it. I suggest that you practice whenever you can.

Keep eye contact with everyone. Here are some places you can practice:

- The bank
- The grocery store
- With your friends and family
- Library
- The park

Here's another tip. If you want to make sure people get the right message from your eye contact, make sure that you smile! If you aren't smiling, the eye contact might be perceived as threatening, and that's the last thing you need!

Wear Bold Colors

Bold colors are great. However, if you aren't careful, you can overdo it. You don't need to have a mélange of clashing colors competing for attention. You don't need to be a peacock! However, you should consider some ways to use color so you can get a bit more attention.

Consider the color of clothing that most people wear, especially to events. They will often choose black, grey, and similar muted, neutral colors. When you add some bright and bold colors, such as with a tie, a handkerchief, or even the frames on your glasses, you can be sure it will get some attention.

A great idea is to tie that color or that "prop" in with your branding in some way. If you have a certain color tie that you wear, or certain colorful shows, you should always wear them to events. It helps you stand out, and once people realize the color or item is your "thing" they may start to recognize you, even though they may never have met you before.

Get Off the Phone

Here is a large problem that's facing quite a bit of our society today. Everyone feels they need to have a constant connection to the web, and that means they are always on their phones. Whether they are checking email, on one of the social networks, or searching for a restaurant, people always have their faces buried in the latest technology.

While the technology can be a great way to keep up with the world, and it can certainly help with branding, it can be a killer when you are trying to meet people in a face-to-face setting. They want to see you – not the back of your phone. When you are at an event, make sure you put the phone down. The web will still be there later.

Posture is Important

How do you carry yourself? Do you sit or walk slouched over and hunched? If you do, it can send a negative message out into the world. When you carry yourself with confidence and good posture that also sends a message. Keeping your head up, your shoulders back, and a smile on your face helps to show that you are confident.

When you slouch and look down at the ground, you will seem as though you lack confidence and even that you are lazy. If you have bad posture, you aren't alone. Many people do, and it often stems from sitting at desks for long hours. It takes some time and some conscious effort on your part, but you can make changes to your posture when you actively try.

Think Positively and with Confidence

There is something to be said for positive thinking. While it might not be magical like The Secret would have you believe, it can do quite a bit for the way you feel and the way others see you.

When they notice that you have a positive attitude, it can help to put them in a positive frame of mind as well. Whenever you are talking about your brand, your life, and your stories, always try to focus on the positive.

Focus on Your Message

By now, you should know your brand and the message that you want to get out to the world. No matter what it is, you should have it distilled in your mind to the essentials. You know the talking points, you know what you want others to learn about your brand, and you know exactly what you want people to come away with after speaking to you at an event.

When you are talking with people, make sure that you are focusing on those things. Focus on your brand, but try not to be overly promotional while you are doing it. Finding this balance can be difficult, but by watching the person's reactions and gauging his or her attention, you can see whether you are going to far or not.

It is generally best to err on the side of caution rather than over-hyping your brand and product and turning them off entirely. A good way to get someone back who is fading as you are talking with them is to ask them a question. This helps them engage with the conversation you are having.

Who Do You Know?

If you know someone at one of the events, that's great. Whether you know the person in real life, or you've only spoken online, having that contact is a great start. You will generally feel more comfortable around that person.

This person may also have contacts at the event that he or she can introduce you do as well. Meeting someone through another person is always a good way to introduce yourself and break the ice.

If you are going to the event with no one you know, look up some information about the other attendees. Find some common ground with them and strike up a conversation. If the event is still a few weeks or months away, connect with the person through social media and start a dialogue before you even get to the event. This is a great way to break the proverbial ice even before you meet.

Matching Your Image to Your Brand

When you are building your brand, you have to think about many different factors. The content you create and the tone of the content are two of the most important ingredients. However, you can't forget the importance of the third ingredient – the image.

The way you present yourself is very important. You do not have to be a model, but you do need to make sure the visual image you project matches your brand. We touched on the importance of this earlier. Steve Job's look matched his brand quite well, and Lady Gaga matches her personal brand perfectly. You need to find out what image will work for the image you want to put out there. Your clothing and your grooming need to match your brand.

Take a moment to think about some celebrities who have unique brands and then switch their grooming and pattern of dress with a completely different celebrity. You will see just how important and powerful branding is and why the look really is important. Let's look at a few examples of how these switches just wouldn't work.

- Switch Zach Galifianakis and Justin Bieber
- Switch Oprah Winfrey and Lindsay Lohan
- Switch Bruce Willis and Michael Cera

Each of these celebrities has his or her successful brand. Their look, and their brand, is so unique to them though that switching just isn't possible – although it is somewhat amusing to consider. Think about this with your own brand. You need to develop your signature brand and look and not simply try to adopt what someone else is doing.

You have your own story and you've been working on what you want your brand to be, so you shouldn't have any trouble doing this!

Great Ways to Communicate Your Brand

You have quite a few tools in your arsenal that can help you. Use this list as a reminder and some inspiration when you are trying to look for new ways to communicate with and build your audience. Bring your content to people in as many ways as possible

- Blogs
- Emails
- Videos
- Podcasts
- Newsletters
- Articles
- Social media
- Speaking engagements
- Write a book
- Make an appearance
- Sponsor an event
- Conduct a workshop online or offline

All of the things you've learned thus far can help you to expand your network and grow your audience. Keep working on ur brand and keep building toward the future.

> **"When you're being your authentic self on social media, people will want to connect with you "**
>
> Jill Celeste,
> Personal
> Branding
> Coach

CHAPTER 11

How to Build a Personal Brand in Your Current Job for More Success

What if you already have a job you enjoy and you want to further your career with that particular company? Personal branding is still one of the best ways to improve your chance of advancing through the ranks. Here are tips that will help you use your brand smartly to help with your career.

Support the Company Mission with the Brand

What is the company's overall mission statement? If you enjoy working for the company, then there is a good chance they already have similar values to you and they have similar overarching goals. By making sure your brand and goals work with those of the company, it is easier to believe in and support what they do.

If your company's values and mission are vastly different from what you want, then you might want to reconsider working their even if the way is good. Remember, you need to be honest to your brand and yourself if you hope to be happy.

Have a Plan

You have to have some type of plan that has attainable and measurable goals. Let people know that you would one day like to move up through the company and learn the path you will have to take to get there. Make sure you follow that path and measure where you are every year or so to see what you might have to do to get there faster. This lets you see if your strategies and brand are working, or if you need to make some changes.

Of course, the speed with which you can advance will differ based on the field you are in most of the time, so consider that when you are developing your plan and goals. You can adjust your plan as needed.

The Right Style – Get Your Style to Work with Your Career Goals

We went over image in the last chapter, but it is important to repeat it here. You have to have the right image for whatever job you want to have. Look at the company culture and make sure the brand you are presenting matches their overall style and aesthetic.

After all, you don't see many powerful attorneys with torn shorts, wild facial hair and an overall disheveled look. Even if he happened to be the best attorney in the world, you would probably be reticent to hire him. Your bosses think the same way no matter what field you are in. If you can't look the part, you don't get the part.

Here is a piece of advice that is always worth following – dress for the job you want to have and not the job you already have. The makes people see you in a different light and it actually can provide you with a career boost.

Consider Your Body Language

Body language is extremely important in how people see you. If you come across as overly aggressive with your body language, or if you seem meek and mousy, it can send the wrong impressions to your managers. Be conscious of your body language and project a confident image.

Watch the Attitude

Everyone probably has at least one or two things about the workplace they don't like, even if it really is the ideal job. Perhaps they don't have the type of food you like in the vending machines in the break room. Maybe they hired another person for the job you wanted.

Whatever type of issues you might have, it is important to make sure you check your attitude while at work. Try to present a positive attitude all of the time and look at the bright side of things. A poor attitude is no small thing, and it can turn managers off from promoting you.

If the problems are actually large, and you can't do anything about them, it might not be the right place for you to work.

Personalize Your Space with Your Brand

Your office or cubicle should be a reflection of your brand. A great way to do this is with color. Use the colors of your brand and logo in your space. For example, if blue is one of the primary colors you use on your site and in your logo, you might want to have some items that utilize that color, such as a painting. If family is important to you – as it is for many people – have a few personal family photos on display.

Books that are in line with your brand and philosophy are a nice touch too. People who come into your workspace should immediately get a sense of who you are, as well as what you are about, when they visit. Combined with your manner of dress and the way you carry yourself, you can brand before you even say a word.

Do the Best Job Possible

While you might want to have a different job in the company eventually, you have to take care of your current work if you hope to advance. Doing a great job in your current task will cement you into the minds of your supervisors and managers. A good company is always on the search for great talent, and they want to hire from within whenever possible. It is more cost effective for them, and it encourages those who are already at the company to work hard in the hopes they can advance.

Try to go beyond what the job requires whenever needed in order to show your commitment. Take classes, learn more about the company, and make it known that you would like to advance.

Connect with the People

You have a wealth of people all around you each day that make the perfect audience for your brand. Your peers and your supervisors are the lifeblood of the business. Connect with them, voice your brand, and build a network of supporters with your peers and supervisors. Make real friendships and relationships. They can serve you well in and out of work now and far into the future.

Think of your workplace like a private social network. Make as many meaningful connections as you can.

> **"If opportunity doesn't knock, build a door."**
>
> Milton Berle

CHAPTER 12

Working with a Personal Branding Specialist Are They Helpful or Harmful?

By now, you've seen that developing and continuing to build your personal brand can be quite a bit of work. In fact, it can often seem like a second job. While many people thrive when it comes to branding themselves, it might be more work than you want to handle on your own. If that's the case, you want to learn more about personal branding specialists.

These specialists have the skills and expertise it takes to make branding much easier for you – they can take care of quite a bit of the hard work. However, that doesn't let you off the hook entirely! You still need to work with them to determine what path the branding should take.

They can take your information and your story and help you with the technical details of what you need to do.

Before you decide to use one of these specialists though, it is a good idea to weigh the pros and cons of what they offer. Learn as much about them as possible and then start looking for someone to help you if you decide the route is the one you want to take with your branding.

The Pros

Personal branding is something that's likely very new for you, and it can be overwhelming. If you have the time and the inclination, you can tackle branding on your own. It is entirely possible to do it without the help of an expert. The specialist can make things so much easier for you though.

The professional has a much better idea of what will work and what will not work since they have actual experience helping other people with their own brand. While you can certainly learn all of these things on your own, a specialist can help to cut the learning curve down quite a bit.

In addition, you will not have to do quite as much of the behind the scenes work. This can leave you more time to work on other things – speaking engagements, books, blogs, etc.

The Cons

Of course, with all of the great things about personal branding specialists, there are some disadvantages as well.

Naturally, you have to pay the specialist, and this might not be in everyone's budget. When you place your brand into the hands of someone else, you are losing a bit of control over it too. If you and the specialist are not on the same page during the development phase of your brand, you could run the risk of putting out the wrong message that does not fit with you or your values.

Therefore, you have to make sure you are working with the right specialist. Otherwise, it could be disastrous.

In addition, unless you have a contract with the specialist, he or she is not bound to working with you. In fact, he or she might work with a competitor after helping you. While legitimate and reputable companies will not divulge information, you still need to be careful.

The consultants generally have to take on several different clients at a single time. This means they are juggling a number of different projects unless you hire them exclusively, and that is expensive. If they have to handle several projects at once, it means they are not giving your brand the full attention it deserves.

If You Choose to Hire a Specialist...

If you want to save some time and effort, and you feel that working with a specialist is the right choice for you, then you need to be cautious when hiring. Here is a list of things you have to do and think about when you are making your decision on which specialist to choose.

- ✅ How much experience do they have?
- ✅ How much time can they spend on your brand?
- ✅ How much will the service cost?
- ✅ What areas of branding help do they offer?
- ✅ Are you and the specialist on the same page with your vision?
- ✅ Can they help grow your brand now and in the future?
- ✅ Do your research. Vet the company and know everything they have to offer before you hire them. It is in your own best interest.

My Recommendation

I honestly feel that working with a specialist is the best way to ensure you are branding the right way. Many people simply don't have the time to do that and do all of the other work they have to do in life. That's entirely understandable.

While I've gone over a number of different techniques and tips that you can use, and I'm confident they will work for you, it really is a substantial amount of work to do on your own.

If you don't have the knowledge or time, you can find a great branding specialist who can make your life quite a bit easier. It's a service I offer, and I'm confident that I can help nearly anyone build a great brand and presence on the web today.

A great branding specialist can look at where you are right now in your branding and can give you an assessment of what you need to do and the strategies you need to employ in order to find success.

Specialists such as myself can take away all of the guesswork and confusion that often surrounds branding today. We can also make sure you are on the cutting-edge of the latest and most important changes in the field of personal branding.

"A personal brand is your promise to the marketplace and the world."

Tom Peters

CHAPTER 13
Avoid These Personal Branding Mistakes

Thus far, we've covered the things that you should be doing with your branding in order to stand out and to grow your audience. Now, it is time we look at some of the things you need to avoid. In this chapter, we will go over the most common and egregious personal branding mistakes.

Be on the lookout for these mistakes in your own efforts now and down the road. Nip them in the bud if you see them starting to creep their way into your branding. If you don't, you will have some trouble.

Inconsistency

You need to be consistent with your brand. People want to know they can trust what you have to say, and staying consistent with the messages you put out from day to day and week to week is important.

If you support something or have a certain value, you can't simply stop supporting it or change your values down the line without having an open dialogue with your audience as to why. If you simply change your tactics without people understanding the reasons behind it, you will come across as inconsistent.

Of course, there are some very good reasons for change. If you are passionate about animals and you find out a company you supported tests product on animals thenstop supporting that company. Just let the audience know why, so they can see that you are being consistent to your overall brand.

Lack of Knowledge

You are trying to brand yourself as an expert, and that means you really do need to be an expert if you hope to grow your target audience, whoever they might be. If your audience has more information and knowledge than you do, then why do they need you? The short answer is they won't need you. You have to make sure you are up to date on all of the latest in your field.

Not Enough Detail about You

You are building a personal brand, and that means people want to know more about you. If you aren't providing them with enough information, they aren't going to trust you or the brand you are trying to develop. Remember all of the work from the earlier chapters. You need to know your values, the identity you want to project, and you need to have a good story. Without them, you are not a brand. You are just another faceless person in a sea of forgettable faces.

Lack of Communication Skills

This can hurt you in two different ways. First, if you aren't putting out enough information and you aren't regularly in front of your target audience, they will not remember you. Second, if you have poor spelling or grammar, or you do not know how to connect with your audience, they will turn away from you.

This is as true for audio and video as it is for written content. It is a good idea to practice and to get better at all of the ways you communicate with your target.

Dishonest and Bad Behavior

This is the real killer for your brand. If your target sees you being dishonest, they will not trust again easily. If you lie about your skills and your knowledge, those things will come back to haunt you. People expect honesty. They also expect a certain level of behavior from you. Poor behavior will reflect negatively most of the time.

If you are trying to get a new job and you've positioned your brand to where you feel you are surely going to get that job, bad behavior seen on social networks, in comments on blogs, and elsewhere can nix your chances in a heartbeat. Remember that in today's world, what you do and say has a chance to get out there, no matter how private you think it might be.

Being Unrealistic

Another problem that some people face is assuming their branding will make them a superstar overnight. Of course, overnight success with branding is not the way things will happen though, at least most of the time. You need to put in the hard work and the time to cultivate your brand if you really want to have a chance at success.

The problem comes from people not seeing that immediate success. Instead of working harder, they immediately try to change their brand. This can do more harm than good many times. Making those changes before you give your branding a change to take hold can be a huge mistake.

You might be on the verge of success and your branding change could actually confuse people. Rebranding is possible, but you shouldn't rebrand without a very good reason. Changing just a few things and refocusing your direction, while keeping the brand much the same is a much better idea.

First, see what you might be able to do different to keep pushing your current brand. Make sure you are focusing on the right people too. You should remember from earlier in the book you have to focus on the right demographic if you want success for your brand.

For example, if you happen to be a true crime writer who wants to find more readers, you wouldn't focus your branding and marketing efforts on finding new readers in a forum on weight loss.

However, connecting with people on true crime websites, and on forums for true crime documentary shows might be a good idea. Know the people you need to reach and focus on finding them.

Only think about rebranding when you are sure the efforts are getting you nowhere!

If you can avoid all of these mistakes and if you work hard, branding success will be in your future. It takes people different amounts of time to reach the levels of success they want, but you can make it.

> **"Success does not consist in never making mistakes but in never making the same one a second time."**
> George Bernard Shaw

"_

CHAPTER 14

Watch Out for Killer Social Networking Mistakes

In the last chapter, we discussed many of the mistakes people trying to build their personal brands often make. One of the things we didn't touch on was social media mishaps. The reason they are absent from the last chapter is because they require an entire chapter of their own!

Check out all of the following mistakes and make sure you don't make them in your social media efforts.

Being Too Pushy

Many companies and individuals with something to promote are guilty of this. They get on the social networks and feel as though it is their own private funnel for marketing – and that's all they do! You never want to come across as too pushy when you are on the social sites. If you are always promoting, people will stop following you, and they could even report you to the site for spamming.

Let people know about what you have going on and any events you might be holding. However, don't make that the only message you put out there!

Not Being Social

This issue ties in with the first mistake quite nicely. You are on a social network. Follow people who follow you, and most importantly, engage with those people so you can build actual relationships. If you don't do this, they will forget about you. You want to spread the influence of your brand and word of mouth is a great way to do that. Make sure you actually connect with people on social media.

Incomplete Profiles

Always complete your profile. Whenever you have the ability to customize your profile, do it. With Twitter, for example, you can change the background. Make sure this matches your brand. Add your personal logo where you can. Fill out your information entirely to give potential followers, friends, and fans as much information about you as possible.

Not Linking

Many people simply forget about this or don't think it is important. Remember that your blog or website is the center of your hub. Social media networks, such as Twitter and Facebook are spokes leading out from that hub. Make sure you link to your social networks from your site, and make sure you have links from your social networks back to your central site. This helps with your SEO as well.

Lack of Focus in Your Messages

Your messages and your content need to have focus. They need to further your brand message in some way. Being personal can be fine depending on the type of brand you are building. However, you don't want to share too much information. You have to keep focus.

For example, if you are trying to position yourself as a leader in the field of forensics, you might not want to talk about your new puppy on your branded social networks. While puppies might be cute, they don't have much to do with forensic science.

Lack of Humility

Braggarts are everywhere in social media. Some people do not even realize they are bragging though. You might fall into this category. When you have good things happen, you want to let others know. However, you must make sure you have a bit of humility when you post. Otherwise, people will start rolling their eyes.

Avoid the outright brag, and avoid the humble brag too. If you force the humility, it really does look as obnoxious as an outright brag.

Be honest. Just let people know what's happening with you and your events without coming across as obnoxious. If you want to let people know about an accomplishment, do that as well. Do not make it appear as though you are trying to draw attention to yourself. Many celebrities do this, and it actually makes them look a bit ridiculous!

In addition, make sure you comment on the successes of other people in your network and those who are not in your network. This shows people that you think about things other than yourself.

"Engage, Enlighten, Encourage and especially...just be yourself! Social media is a community effort, everyone is an asset."

Susan Cooper

CHAPTER 15
Tips to Help You Keep Building Your Brand into the Future

You should have a good idea of how to start building your personal brand by now. You are determining your brand positioning and you are working on your story so you can target the perfect audience. Once you launch your brand though, you can't simply rest on your laurels. You need to keep working and building your brand if you hope to keep growing it into the future.

In this chapter, we will cover some of the best ways to make sure your personal brand gains strength and recognition in the years to come.

Keep Up with the Times and Tech

Times change and so does technology. A decade ago, social networks were not what they are today. Websites, blogs, and tools were far different and what we might even call "primitive" by today's standards. Today's technology will feel just as outdated in a few years. Make sure you always keep up with the times so you can keep up with your audience!

Keep Looking at the Competition

Never stop watching what the competition is doing. Keep looking for competitors, new and old, to see what they are doing and what they are offering. When your competitors make changes to the way they are reaching their audiences, or they make changes in the services they offer, you need to pay attention.

Take on the Best Projects

The goal of building a great personal brand is to make sure you have the opportunities to take on the jobs and the projects that appeal to you the most. Keep taking on new and challenging projects and jobs. This can keep your brand growing and moving forward into the future.

Create New Goals

Never be satisfied with the status quo. You want to grow as a person, and you want new opportunities. This means you need to reevaluate your plan occasionally so you can create new goals to reach. Having goals gives you something on which you can place your focus. When you write those goals down and take active steps in reaching them, you are more likely to succeed.

Nurture Your Audience

You spend time and effort to build your audience. You don't want to leave them in the lurch once you have them! Nurture your connections by keeping in contact with them. Keep them updated on what you are doing and listen to their questions and suggestions.

Stay as current as possible with social networks along with whatever changes come to them in the future. Make sure you

remember to connect with your audience both online and offline for the maximum effect for your brand.

"Personal branding is about unearthing what is true and unique about you and letting everyone know about it."

Dan Schawbel

Conclusion

Throughout this book, we've looked at everything from the importance of personal branding to how you can build your own powerful brand. The tips, tools, and techniques in this book should help you to develop your own strong and successful brand.

At the outset, it might seem hard to create your own, but it is entirely possible, and it can be fun to do. You have the tools and knowledge you need, and you have your unique story that will help to make you unique. It takes some work, but no one knows you better than you!

Take the tools and the guidelines presented here and tweak them for your own needs. Start building your brand right now.

But first...

Back to Google

Do you remember when we talked about Googling your name at the beginning of this book? Do you recall your results?

Chances are the items that popped up in your results were not giving people the best first impression of you.

Now that you've done all of this work though, it's time that you went back to the search engine and did it all over again. Type your name into the search engine and see what comes up.

By now, you should have taken all – or at least most – of the steps in this book and employed them. This means that you should start to see a definite change in the types of results that come up when you search for your name. You should now be finding results that you want and the results that best represent who you are and what you can offer.

If you don't see drastic results, don't worry quite yet. It takes some time for everything to propagate through the web and for those changes to take real hold. You should be able to see a difference within the first couple of weeks though, and surely within the first month, as long as you are dedicated and you keep up with all of your blogging, social networking, and more.

Real Change and a Powerful Brand

Use the guidance and tools in this book. Seek the help of a great mentor who can actually show you just what you need to do to build your brand to its full potential, and keep working. You have the power to make these changes, so get started right now!

Key Terms and Glossary

Branding has a number of specialized terms and words that you are likely to come across, many of which you've probably seen in this book thus far.

The following is a handy list of some of the terms that are common in the field. You don't have to commit them to memory, but it can be helpful to know what each of them means.

Important terms to know in the field of branding:

- **Awareness** – How many people or employers in your target demographic are aware of your existence? The greater the awareness of your brand the better you can do.

- **Brand** – A brand is the image you project. It is a combination of a number of different things, some tangible and some intangible. It is a way to let the world know who you are and what you believe. Branding can take a number of forms. It can be corporate branding, such as you would find with a company such as Goodyear, or it can be personal branding, that you might see in celebrities such as Michael Jordan.

✅ **Brand Platform** – The platform for a brand will contain a number of different features and elements, including your vision, your values, your mission, your personality, and your overall tone.

✅ **Branded Resume** – a specialized resume that reflects your personal brand to show your uniqueness and perfectness for the job, and to help you stand apart from the competition.

✅ **Co-Branding** – The use of more than just one name in an effort to support a new service or product. Two different personal brands may come together in this fashion, just as two corporate brands can.

✅ **Core Competencies** – These are your areas of strength and skill, the things you bring to your personal brand that can help it to succeed.

✅ **Demographics** – Just as with corporate branding, individuals need to be aware of the demographics of their audience. Some of the things to consider may include age, nationality, education, and income.

✅ **Ghostwriter** – If you want to write a book, but you don't have the time, inclination, or ability to do it on your own, you can always hire a ghostwriter, who will write the book for you. You pay a flat fee, and you get to put your name on the book.

✅ **Intangibles** –The things that you can't touch, but are a part of the overall brand. This could be a logo, the color scheme a company's website and literature, and even copyrights. These can apply to personal branding as well. For example, J.K. Rowling is best known for her work on Harry Potter. The copyrights and trademarks might be intangible, but they are certainly a part of her personal branding.

✅ **Internal Brand Building** – Building your brand from inside out. This is the case with most personal brands – they are a reflection of the person that hopefully becomes greater than the individual alone.

✓ **Mission** – The overall goals of your personal brand. The mission is what you hope to accomplish, and most people have several missions – short-term and long-term goals.

✓ **Logo**– A graphic design or symbol used to identify a company or organization. Some great examples of easily recognizable logos include Superman's "S", the golden arches of McDonalds, and the Playboy Bunny. While companies are the ones that generally utilize logos, it is possible for individuals to adopt logos for their personal branding as well.

✓ **Niche** – A niche is your specialty, an area of expertise that helps to make you important to a certain subset of people or employers. The narrower your niche, the smaller your audience may be, but the audience will be perfect for what you can offer.

✓ **Offline Branding** – Techniques for spreading the influence of your brand in the offline world, such as trade shows, conventions, meetings. Traditional articles in magazines, on television, and on the radio can act as offline branding tools as well.

✓ **Online Branding** – Techniques use to spread the influence of your brand online, such as blogging and social networks.

✓ **Personal Branding Statement** – The one or two sentence description of you and your brand. You can think of this as an encapsulated biography that can incorporate your values, views, and goals succinctly.

✓ **Psychographics** – This looks at the lifestyles of potential clients or customers to give you more insight into their interests, likes, and dislikes.

✅ **Rebranding** – Sometimes you may find that your brand simply isn't generating the amount of attention, or the kind of attention, that you want and need. In these cases, it is advisable to look at your plan again and rethink your strategy. Changing your brand, or rebranding, is possible.

✅ **SEO** – Stands for Search Engine Optimization. Important for helping people find your site and your brand online.

✅ **Social Media** – Social media is an inescapable necessity of life today for individuals as well as businesses. Some of the most popular social media networks today include LinkedIn, Facebook, and Twitter. They are essential for personal branding.

✅ **Speaker Bureau** – A bureau is similar to an agency, and they can help book engagements for speakers. This leaves you to handle other aspects of your life while they take care of the booking details.

✅ **Story** – Great stories help to connect with your audience on an emotional level. They need to be honest, have a full story arc (beginning/middle/end), and they need to be entertaining.

✅ **SWOT** – An acronym that stands for Strengths, Weaknesses, Opportunities, and Threats.

Tangibles – These are things that you can touch, such as clothing or other elements that make you and your brand stand out. It could be something such as Steve Jobs' sweaters or Tiger Woods' red shirt.

✅ **Target** – Your target audience is the group of people you want to know more about you and what you have to offer. Your target could be potential employers, clients, or even people working in your current organization.

✅ **Values** – Your values are the things you hold to be important when it comes to living your life. They can affect how you deal with other people and how people see you.

About The Author

Mark Cijo is a Digital Marketing Consultant, Mentor & Speaker based out of Dubai, UAE. He is the Co-Founder of Brawnycode, a Digital Marketing Agency based in India.

With an educational background in Computer Science, Mathematics and Physics from reputable universities, Mark's exposure to and knowledge of the internet is second to none. Combined with his inquisitive nature and drive to succeed, Mark has become a leading authority in digital inbound marketing. Having expertise in the fields of brand building, coaching and mentoring (among many others) has already opened up many opportunities for Mark and has taken him around the world - from Dubai to Australia, India to the UK.

Mark has had over 8 years of experience in the digital marketing industry, a career which has been imbued with success and accolades. Not only has he worked with some of the largest life science, wellness and ecommerce companies in the world, he was invited to be a panelist for the 5th GCC Smart Government and Cities Portals Conference held in Dubai in 2013.

Having had stunning personal success, he discovered a new passion of his - helping others achieve this level of success for themselves.

No one knows better than Mark does the importance of branding and marketing to any company. As such, he offers mentoring, training and consultation services to businesses and executives all over the world. In his career he has helped innumerable businesses implement highly successful marketing strategies at highly competitive rates, leading many clients of his to hail him as a "God send".

Website: www.markcijo.com
Email: markcijo@gmail.com
Facebook: www.facebook.com/markcijo-fb

33811658R00135

Made in the USA
Lexington, KY
15 July 2014